W9-CEO-875

Full Color on Every Page!

Computers Simplified®

5th Edition

Visual

From
maranGraphics™

&

IDG Books Worldwide, Inc.
An International Data Group Company
Foster City, CA • Chicago, IL • Indianapolis, IN • New York, NY

Computers Simplified® 5th Edition

Published by
IDG Books Worldwide, Inc.
An International Data Group Company
919 E. Hillsdale Blvd., Suite 300
Foster City, CA 94404
(650) 653-7000

Library of Congress Catalog Card No.: 00-107998

ISBN: 0-7645-3524-2

Printed in the United States of America

10 9 8 7 6 5 4 3 2 1

5K/QT/RS/QQ/MG

Distributed in the United States by IDG Books Worldwide, Inc.
Distributed by CDG Books Canada Inc. for Canada; by Transworld Publishers Limited in the United Kingdom; by IDG Norge Books for Norway; by IDG Sweden Books for Sweden; by IDG Books Australia Publishing Corporation Pty. Ltd. for Australia and New Zealand; by TransQuest Publishers Pte Ltd. for Singapore, Malaysia, Thailand, Indonesia, and Hong Kong; by Gotop Information Inc. for Taiwan; by ICG Muse, Inc. for Japan; by Intersoft for South Africa; by Eyrolles for France; by International Thomson Publishing for Germany, Austria and Switzerland; by Distribuidora Cuspide for Argentina; by LR International for Brazil; by Galileo Libros for Chile; by Ediciones ZETA S.C.R. Ltda. for Peru; by WS Computer Publishing Corporation, Inc. for the Philippines; by Contemporanea de Ediciones for Venezuela; by Express Computer Distributors for the Caribbean and West Indies; by Micronesia Media Distributor, Inc. for Micronesia; by Chips Computadoras S.A. de C.V. for Mexico; by Editorial Norma de Panama S.A. for Panama; by American Bookshops for Finland.
For corporate orders, please call maranGraphics at 800-469-6616.
For general information on IDG Books Worldwide's books in the U.S., please call our Consumer Customer Service department at 800-762-2974.
For reseller information, including discounts and premium sales, please call our Reseller Customer Service department at 800-434-3422.
For information on where to purchase IDG Books Worldwide's books outside the U.S., please contact our International Sales department at 317-572-3993 or fax 317-572-4002.
For consumer information on foreign language translations, please contact our Customer Service department at 800-434-3422, fax 800-550-2747, or e-mail rights@idgbooks.com.
For information on licensing foreign or domestic rights, please phone 650-653-7000 or fax 650-653-7500.
For sales inquiries and special prices for bulk quantities, please contact our Sales department at 650-655-3200.
For information on using IDG Books Worldwide's books in the classroom or for ordering examination copies, please contact our Educational Sales department at 800-434-2086 or fax 317-572-4005.
For press review copies, author interviews, or other publicity information, please contact our Public Relations department at 650-653-7000 or fax 650-653-7500.
For authorization to photocopy items for corporate, personal, or educational use, please contact maranGraphics at 800-469-6616.

Trademark Acknowledgments

Permissions

ABOUT IDG BOOKS WORLDWIDE

Welcome to the world of IDG Books Worldwide.

IDG Books Worldwide, Inc., is a subsidiary of International Data Group, the world's largest publisher of computer-related information and the leading global provider of information services on information technology. IDG was founded more than 30 years ago by Patrick J. McGovern and now employs more than 9,000 people worldwide. IDG publishes more than 290 computer publications in over 75 countries. More than 90 million people read one or more IDG publications each month.

Launched in 1990, IDG Books Worldwide is today the #1 publisher of best-selling computer books in the United States. We are proud to have received eight awards from the Computer Press Association in recognition of editorial excellence and three from Computer Currents' First Annual Readers' Choice Awards. Our best-selling ...For Dummies® series has more than 50 million copies in print with translations in 31 languages. IDG Books Worldwide, through a joint venture with IDG's Hi-Tech Beijing, became the first U.S. publisher to publish a computer book in the People's Republic of China. In record time, IDG Books Worldwide has become the first choice for millions of readers around the world who want to learn how to better manage their businesses.

Our mission is simple: Every one of our books is designed to bring extra value and skill-building instructions to the reader. Our books are written by experts who understand and care about our readers. The knowledge base of our editorial staff comes from years of experience in publishing, education, and journalism — experience we use to produce books to carry us into the new millennium. In short, we care about books, so we attract the best people. We devote special attention to details such as audience, interior design, use of icons, and illustrations. And because we use an efficient process of authoring, editing, and desktop publishing our books electronically, we can spend more time ensuring superior content and less time on the technicalities of making books.

You can count on our commitment to deliver high-quality books at competitive prices on topics you want to read about. At IDG Books Worldwide, we continue in the IDG tradition of delivering quality for more than 30 years. You'll find no better book on a subject than one from IDG Books Worldwide.

John Kilcullen
Chairman and CEO
IDG Books Worldwide, Inc.

Eighth Annual
Computer Press
Awards ➤1992

Ninth Annual
Computer Press
Awards ➤1993

Tenth Annual
Computer Press
Awards ➤1994

Eleventh Annual
Computer Press
Awards ➤1995

IDG is the world's leading IT media, research and exposition company. Founded in 1964, IDG had 1997 revenues of $2.05 billion and has more than 9,000 employees worldwide. IDG offers the widest range of media options that reach IT buyers in 75 countries representing 95% of worldwide IT spending. IDG's diverse product and services portfolio spans six key areas including print publishing, online publishing, expositions and conferences, market research, education and training, and global marketing services. More than 90 million people read one or more of IDG's 290 magazines and newspapers, including IDG's leading global brands — Computerworld, PC World, Network World, Macworld and the Channel World family of publications. IDG Books Worldwide is one of the fastest-growing computer book publishers in the world, with more than 700 titles in 36 languages. The "...For Dummies®" series alone has more than 50 million copies in print. IDG offers online users the largest network of technology-specific Web sites around the world through IDG.net (http://www.idg.net), which comprises more than 225 targeted Web sites in 55 countries worldwide. International Data Corporation (IDC) is the world's largest provider of information technology data, analysis and consulting, with research centers in over 41 countries and more than 400 research analysts worldwide. IDG World Expo is a leading producer of more than 168 globally branded conferences and expositions in 35 countries including E3 (Electronic Entertainment Expo), Macworld Expo, ComNet, Windows World Expo, ICE (Internet Commerce Expo), Agenda, DEMO, and Spotlight. IDG's training subsidiary, ExecuTrain, is the world's largest computer training company, with more than 230 locations worldwide and 785 training courses. IDG Marketing Services helps industry-leading IT companies build international brand recognition by developing global integrated marketing programs via IDG's print, online and exposition products worldwide. Further information about the company can be found at www.idg.com. 1/26/00

maranGraphics is a family-run business located near Toronto, Canada.

At **maranGraphics**, we believe in producing great computer books–one book at a time.

Each maranGraphics book uses the award-winning communication process that we have been developing over the last 25 years. Using this process, we organize screen shots, text and illustrations in a way that makes it easy for you to learn new concepts and tasks.

We spend hours deciding the best way to perform each task, so you don't have to! Our clear, easy-to-follow screen shots and instructions walk you through each task from beginning to end.

Our detailed illustrations go hand-in-hand with the text to help reinforce the information. Each illustration is a labor of love–some take up to a week to draw!

We want to thank you for purchasing what we feel are the best computer books money can buy. We hope you enjoy using this book as much as we enjoyed creating it!

Sincerely,

The Maran Family

Please visit us on the Web at:
www.maran.com

Credits

Authors:
Ruth Maran
Paul Whitehead

Copy Editors:
Cathy Benn
Roxanne Van Damme

Project Manager:
Judy Maran

Editors:
Teri Lynn Pinsent
Roderick Anatalio
James Menzies

Layout Designer & Illustrator:
Treena Lees

Illustrators:
Russ Marini
Sean Johannesen
Steven Schaerer
Suzana G. Miokovic
Dave Thornhill
Natalie Tweedie

Indexer:
Roderick Anatalio

Permissions Coordinator:
Jennifer Amaral

Senior Vice President and Publisher, IDG Books Technology Publishing Group:
Richard Swadley

Publishing Director, IDG Books Technology Publishing Group:
Barry Pruett

Editorial Support, IDG Books Technology Publishing Group:
Martine Edwards
Lindsay Sandman
Sandy Rodrigues

Post Production:
Robert Maran

Acknowledgments

Thanks to the dedicated staff of maranGraphics, including Jennifer Amaral, Roderick Anatalio, Cathy Benn, Sean Johannesen, Kelleigh Johnson, Wanda Lawrie, Luis Lee, Treena Lees, Jill Maran, Judy Maran, Robert Maran, Ruth Maran, Russ Marini, James Menzies, Suzana G. Miokovic, Stacey Morrison, Teri Lynn Pinsent, Steven Schaerer, Norm Schumacher, Raquel Scott, Dave Thornhill, Natalie Tweedie, Roxanne Van Damme and Paul Whitehead.

Finally, to Richard Maran who originated the easy-to-use graphic format of this guide. Thank you for your inspiration and guidance.

Table of Contents

CHAPTER 3

PROCESSING

CHAPTER 4

STORAGE DEVICES

CHAPTER 5

SOFTWARE

CHAPTER 6

OPERATING SYSTEMS . . . .

Table of Contents

CHAPTER 1

INTRODUCTION TO COMPUTERS

Do you want to learn more about your computer? This chapter will help you get started.

HARDWARE AND SOFTWARE

Hardware and software are the two basic parts of a computer system.

HARDWARE

Hardware is any part of a computer system you can see or touch.

Peripheral

A peripheral is any piece of hardware attached to a computer, such as a printer.

SOFTWARE

Software is a set of electronic instructions that tell a computer what to do. You cannot see or touch software, but you can see and touch the packaging the software comes in.

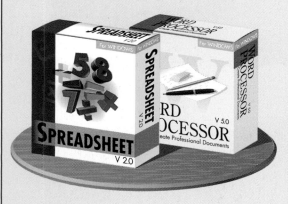

Application Software

Application software allows you to accomplish specific tasks. Popular application software includes Microsoft Word and Intuit Quicken.

Operating System Software

Operating system software controls the overall activity of a computer. Most new computers come with the Windows Me operating system software.

GETTING HELP

There are many ways to get help when using new hardware and software.

DOCUMENTATION

Hardware and software should include documentation that tells you how to set up and use the product. Many software packages also come with a built-in help feature. You should check local book stores for manuals with detailed, step-by-step instructions.

CONSULT THE EXPERTS

If you have questions about setting up or using new hardware or software, try calling the store where you purchased the product. You can also visit the manufacturer's Web site on the Internet for more information about the product.

CLASSES

Colleges and computer stores often offer computer courses. Many communities also have computer clubs where you can ask questions and exchange ideas.

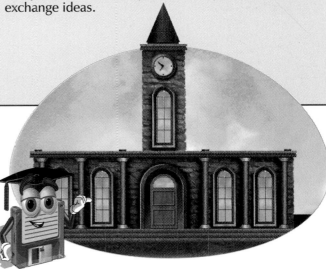

HOW COMPUTERS WORK

A computer collects, processes, stores and outputs information.

INPUT

An input device lets you communicate with a computer. You can use input devices to enter information and issue commands. A keyboard, mouse and joystick are input devices.

PROCESS

The Central Processing Unit (CPU) is the main chip in a computer. The CPU processes instructions, performs calculations and manages the flow of information through a computer system. The CPU communicates with input, output and storage devices to perform tasks.

STORE

A storage device is used to place information on storage media. The computer uses information stored on the storage media to perform tasks. Popular examples of storage devices include a hard drive, floppy drive, CD-R drive, tape drive and DVD-ROM drive.

OUTPUT

An output device lets a computer communicate with you. These devices display information on a screen, create printed copies or generate sound. A monitor, printer and speakers are output devices.

Bytes are used to measure the amount of information a device can store.

Byte

One byte is one character. A character can be a number, letter or symbol. One byte consists of eight bits (binary digits). A bit is the smallest unit of information a computer can process.

Kilobyte (KB)

One kilobyte is 1,024 characters. This is approximately equal to one page of double-spaced text.

LIBRARY

Megabyte (MB)

One megabyte is 1,048,576 characters. This is approximately equal to one book.

Gigabyte (GB)

One gigabyte is 1,073,741,824 characters. This is approximately equal to a shelf of books in a library.

Terabyte (TB)

One terabyte is 1,099,511,627,776 characters. This is approximately equal to an entire library of books.

TYPES OF COMPUTER SYSTEMS

There are several types of computer systems.

PC (PERSONAL COMPUTER)

A PC is a computer designed to meet the needs of an individual and usually refers to IBM-compatible computers. PCs are found in many businesses and are popular for home use.

MACINTOSH

Macintosh computers are found in many homes and are very popular in the graphics, publishing and multimedia industries. The Macintosh was the first home computer that offered a graphical display.

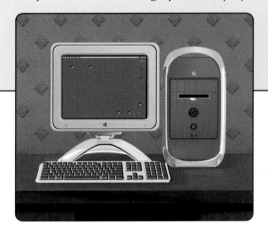

MAINFRAME

A mainframe is a computer that can process and store large amounts of information and support many users at the same time. A terminal, consisting of a keyboard and monitor, is used to input and output information on a mainframe.

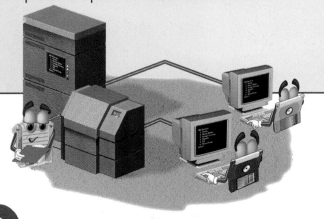

SET-TOP BOX

A set-top box is a computer device that connects to your television. Set-top boxes allow you to use your telephone line or cable connection to browse the Internet and exchange electronic mail on your television.

A TYPICAL COMPUTER

A typical computer system consists of several parts.

Monitor

A monitor is a device that displays text and images generated by the computer.

Printer

A printer is a device that produces a paper copy of documents you create on the computer.

Computer Case

A computer case contains the major components of a computer system.

Speakers

Speakers are devices that play sound generated by a computer.

Modem

A modem is a device that lets computers communicate through telephone lines. A modem can be found inside or outside the computer case.

Keyboard

A keyboard is a device that lets you type information and instructions into a computer.

Mouse

A mouse is a handheld device that lets you select and move items on the screen.

Power Supply

A power supply changes normal household electricity into electricity that a computer can use.

Hard Drive

A hard drive is the primary device that a computer uses to store information.

Port

A port is a connector where you plug in an external device such as a printer.

Expansion Card

An expansion card lets you add new features to a computer. For example, an expansion card can give a computer the ability to record and play sound.

Expansion Slot

An expansion slot is a socket on the system board. An expansion card plugs into an expansion slot.

System Board

A system board is the main circuit board of a computer. All electrical components plug into the system board.

All computers contain the same basic components.

CD-ROM or DVD-ROM Drive

A CD-ROM drive reads information stored on Compact Discs (CDs). A DVD-ROM drive reads information stored on CDs and Digital Versatile Discs (DVDs).

Floppy Drive

A floppy drive stores and retrieves information on floppy disks.

Drive Bay

A drive bay is a space inside the computer case where a hard drive, floppy drive, CD-ROM drive or DVD-ROM drive sits.

Central Processing Unit (CPU)

A CPU is the main chip in a computer. The CPU processes instructions, performs calculations and manages the flow of information through a computer.

Random Access Memory (RAM)

RAM temporarily stores information inside a computer. This information is lost when you turn off the computer.

COMPUTER CASE

A computer case contains the major components of a computer system.

Desktop Case

A desktop case usually sits on a desk, under a monitor.

Tower Case

A tower case usually sits on the floor. This provides more desk space, but can be less convenient for inserting and removing items such as floppy disks and CD-ROM discs. Tower cases come in different sizes.

PORTABLE

A portable is a small, lightweight computer that you can easily transport. A portable computer has a built-in keyboard and screen.

ALL-IN-ONE CASE

An all-in-one case contains a monitor, hard drive, CD-ROM drive and speakers in a single unit.

POWER SUPPLY

A power supply changes the alternating current (AC) that comes from an outlet to the direct current (DC) that a computer can use.

The capacity of a power supply is measured in watts. An average computer uses up to 250 watts, whereas an average light bulb uses 60 watts.

A fan inside the power supply prevents the parts inside a computer from overheating.

PROTECT YOUR EQUIPMENT

Changes in electrical power can damage equipment and information.

Surge Protector

A surge protector, or surge suppressor, guards a computer against surges. A surge is a fluctuation in power. These fluctuations happen most often during storms.

UPS

An Uninterruptible Power Supply (UPS) protects a computer from a loss of power. A UPS contains a battery that stores electrical power. If the power fails, the battery can run the computer for a short time so you can save your information.

A port is a connector at the back of a computer where you plug in an external device such as a printer. This allows instructions and data to flow between the computer and the device.

Parallel Port

A parallel port has 25 holes. This type of port is known as a female connector. A parallel port usually connects a printer or an external storage device.

A computer internally labels each parallel port with the letters LPT. The first parallel port is named LPT1, the second parallel port is named LPT2, and so on.

Monitor Port

A monitor port connects a monitor.

Mouse Port

A mouse port connects a mouse.

Keyboard Port

A keyboard port connects a keyboard. A keyboard port can come in two sizes.

Serial Port

A serial port has either 9 or 25 pins. This type of port is known as a male connector. A serial port can connect a mouse or external modem.

A computer internally labels each serial port with the letters COM. The first serial port is named COM1, the second serial port is named COM2, and so on.

Game Port

A game port connects a joystick or other game controller.

Network Port

A network port is found on a network interface card and allows you to connect the computer to a network.

USB Port

Universal Serial Bus (USB) is a type of port that allows you to connect up to 127 devices using only one port. For example, you can use a USB port to connect a printer, modem, joystick and scanner to your computer. Most new computers come with two USB ports.

EXPANSION CARD

An expansion card is a circuit board that lets you add new features to a computer.

An expansion card is also called an expansion board.

EXPANSION SLOT

An expansion slot is a socket where you plug in an expansion card.

The number of expansion slots your computer has affects the number of features you can add to the computer. Before you buy a computer, make sure it has enough empty expansion slots for your future needs.

CONNECT DEVICES

Some expansion cards are accessible from the back of a computer. These expansion cards contain ports where you can plug in devices. For example, you can plug speakers into a sound card to hear the sound generated by the computer.

A computer usually comes with one or more expansion cards.

TYPES OF EXPANSION CARDS

Video

A video card generates the images displayed on the monitor.

Modem

A modem card lets computers exchange information through telephone lines.

Sound

A sound card lets a computer play and record high-quality sound.

Network Interface

A network interface card lets connected computers share information and equipment.

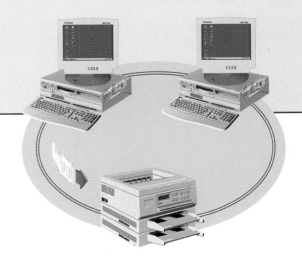

PURCHASE A NEW COMPUTER

You should purchase a computer from a business with a good reputation that has been in operation for a number of years.

CONSIDERATIONS

Cost

The cost of a computer depends on your needs. You can purchase a basic home computer for under $800. If you want a computer better able to handle complex tasks, such as running multimedia applications, you will need to spend more money.

In many cases, a monitor is not included in the price of a computer.

Brand-name and Clone Computers

When purchasing a new computer, you can choose either a brand-name or a clone computer. Brand-name computers are made by large manufacturers, such as IBM or Apple. Clone computers are made by independent manufacturers. Clone computers function exactly like brand-name computers, but are usually less expensive.

After-sale Service

You should make sure the computer you purchase comes with after-sale service. After-sale service should include a one or two-year warranty on computer parts and labor, as well as telephone technical support.

UPGRADE A COMPUTER

You can upgrade a computer to enhance the computer's performance. For many upgrades, you will need the assistance of an experienced computer repairperson.

Upgrading usually refers to replacing an old or obsolete component with a newer component to improve the efficiency of the computer. Upgrading can also include adding a new component, such as a tape drive or DVD-ROM drive, to increase the capabilities of the computer.

CONSIDERATIONS

Cost

You should always determine the cost of an upgrade before performing the upgrade. If you are planning a major upgrade, such as replacing the system board or CPU, it may be less expensive to purchase a new computer.

Effective Upgrades

Increasing the amount of memory in a computer is one of the most effective upgrades you can perform. Doubling the existing memory in a computer can significantly increase the performance of the computer.

CHAPTER 2

INPUT AND OUTPUT

What is a high-speed Internet connection and why would you want one? What type of printer is best for you? This chapter will answer these questions and more.

TOC

A mouse is a handheld device that lets you select and move items on your screen.

A mouse can come in various shapes, colors and sizes.

USE THE MOUSE

Resting your hand on the mouse, use your thumb and two rightmost fingers to move the mouse on the desk. Use your two remaining fingers to press the mouse buttons.

When you move the mouse on your desk, the pointer on the screen moves in the same direction. The pointer assumes different shapes (example: $\&$ or I) depending on its location on the screen and the task you are performing.

MOUSE PAD

A mouse pad provides a smooth surface for moving a mouse and reduces the amount of dirt that enters the mouse. You can buy mouse pads displaying interesting designs or pictures at most computer stores. Some mouse pads have built-in wrist support for increased comfort.

MOUSE ACTIONS

Click

A click often selects an item on the screen. To click, press and release the left mouse button.

Double-click

A double-click often opens a document or starts a program. To double-click, quickly press and release the left mouse button twice.

Right-click

A right-click often displays a list of commands on the screen. To right-click, press and release the right mouse button.

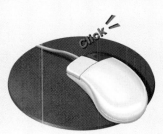

Drag and Drop

Dragging and dropping makes it easy to move an item on the screen. Position the pointer over an item on the screen and then press and hold down the left mouse button. Still holding down the button, move the pointer to where you want to place the item and then release the button.

LEFT-HANDED USERS

If you are left-handed, you can switch the functions of the left and right mouse buttons to make the mouse easier to use. For example, to click an item, you would press the right button instead of the left.

CLEAN THE MOUSE

If there is a ball inside your mouse, you should occasionally remove and clean the ball. Make sure you also remove dust and dirt from the inside to help ensure smooth motion of the mouse.

MOUSE

There are several advanced mouse types available that offer useful features.

ADVANCED MOUSE TYPES

Wheeled Mouse

A wheeled mouse has a wheel between the left and right mouse buttons. You can often use this wheel to scroll through information or zoom in and out. The Microsoft IntelliMouse is a popular example of a wheeled mouse.

Wireless Mouse

A wireless, or cordless, mouse runs on a battery and reduces the clutter on your desk by eliminating the mouse cord. When you move the mouse on your desk, the mouse sends signals to your computer, the same way a remote control sends signals to a television.

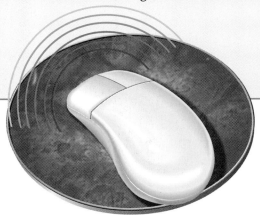

Programmable Mouse

You can purchase a mouse that has buttons you can program to perform specific tasks, such as double-clicking an item. A three-button mouse is an example of a programmable mouse.

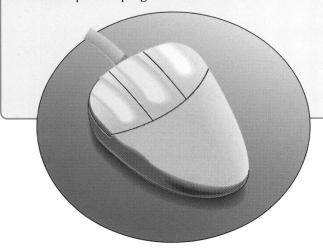

Optical Sensor Mouse

An optical sensor mouse detects mouse movement using an optical sensor rather than a ball inside the mouse. This type of mouse does not contain any moving parts that can wear out or stick. A mouse pad is not required when using an optical sensor mouse.

OTHER POINTING DEVICES

Touchpad

A touchpad is a surface that is sensitive to pressure and motion. When you move your fingertip across the pad, the pointer on the screen moves in the same direction.

Trackball

A trackball is an upside-down mouse that remains stationary on your desk. You roll the ball with your fingers or palm to move the pointer on the screen. A trackball is a great alternative to a mouse when you have limited desk space.

Pointing Stick

A pointing stick resembles the eraser on the end of a pencil. The mouse pointer moves in the direction you push the pointing stick. Pointing sticks also have buttons, similar to mouse buttons, you can press to perform an action such as a click.

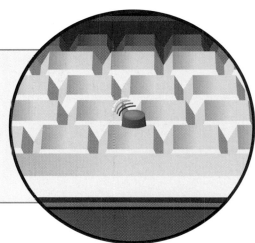

The keys on a keyboard let you enter information and instructions into a computer. Most keyboards have 101 keys. Your keyboard may look different than the keyboard shown here.

Function Keys

These keys let you quickly perform specific tasks. For example, in many programs you can press **F1** to display help information.

Escape Key

You can press **Esc** to quit a task you are performing.

Caps Lock and Shift Keys

These keys let you enter text in uppercase (ABC) and lowercase (abc) letters.

Press **Caps Lock** to change the case of all letters you type. Press the key again to return to the original case.

Press **Shift** in combination with another key to type an uppercase letter.

Ctrl and Alt Keys

You can use the **Ctrl** or **Alt** key in combination with another key to perform a specific task. For example, in some programs you can press **Ctrl** and **S** to save a document.

Windows Key

You can press the **Windows** key to quickly display the Start menu when using a Windows operating system, such as Windows Me or Windows 2000.

Spacebar

You can press the **Spacebar** to insert a blank space.

Backspace Key

You can press **Backspace** to remove the character to the left of the cursor.

Delete Key

You can press **Delete** to remove the character to the right of the cursor.

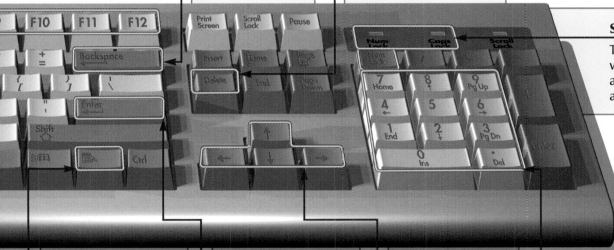

Status Lights

These lights indicate whether the **Num Lock** and **Caps Lock** features are on or off.

Application Key

You can press the **Application** key to quickly display the shortcut menu for an item on your screen.

Enter Key

You can press **Enter** to tell the computer to carry out a task. In a word processing program, press this key to start a new paragraph.

Arrow Keys

These keys let you move the cursor around the screen.

Numeric Keypad

When the **Num Lock** light is on, you can use the number keys (0 through 9) to enter numbers. When the **Num Lock** light is off, you can use these keys to move the cursor around the screen. To turn the light on or off, press **Num Lock**.

A printer produces a paper copy of the information displayed on the screen.

You can buy a printer that produces black-and-white or color images.

You can use a printer to produce letters, invoices, newsletters, transparencies, labels, packing slips and much more.

CHOOSE A PRINTER

There are several factors to consider when buying a printer.

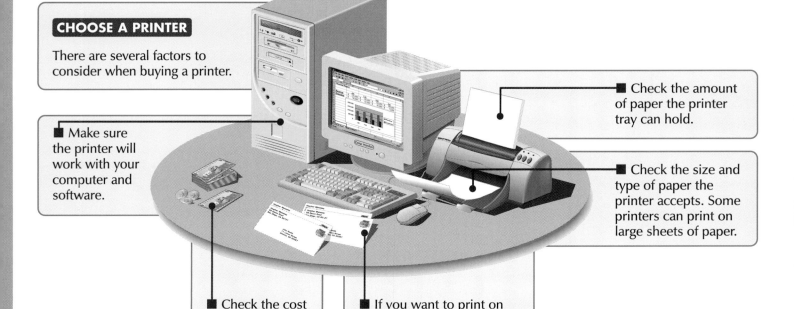

■ Make sure the printer will work with your computer and software.

■ Check the cost of materials such as ink and paper.

■ If you want to print on envelopes, transparencies or labels, make sure the printer will accept these items.

■ Check the amount of paper the printer tray can hold.

■ Check the size and type of paper the printer accepts. Some printers can print on large sheets of paper.

PRINTER SPEED

The speed of a printer determines how quickly it can print pages. Speed is measured in pages per minute (ppm). A higher speed results in faster output.

tic tic tic

A complicated page, such as a page that contains images, takes longer to print than a page containing only text.

PRINTER RESOLUTION

The resolution of a printer determines the quality of the images it can produce. A higher resolution results in sharper, more detailed images.

Printer resolution is measured in dots per inch (dpi). Generally, a resolution of 600 dpi is acceptable for most text documents. 1200 dpi printers are better for printing images.

600 dpi

1200 dpi

Resolution can also be expressed with two numbers (example: 600 x 600 dpi). These numbers describe the number of dots a printer can produce across and down one square inch.

INK-JET PRINTER

An ink-jet printer produces high-quality documents at a relatively low price. This type of printer is ideal for routine business and personal documents.

An ink-jet printer has a print head that sprays ink through small nozzles onto a page.

Speed

Most ink-jet printers produce images at a speed of 2 to 10 pages per minute (ppm).

Maximum 10 ppm

Resolution

The resolution, or quality, of the images produced by an ink-jet printer ranges from 360 to 2400 dots per inch (dpi).

360 dpi

2400 dpi

Ink

Ink-jet printers use ink stored in cartridges. When the ink runs out, you replace the cartridge. You may also be able to refill a cartridge with ink. You should always use the printer manufacturer's recommended cartridges or ink for best results.

Many ink cartridges have an expiry date on them. Before you buy a new cartridge, you should make sure it has not expired.

Paper

Ink-jet printers accept 8 1/2 by 11-inch paper. Some ink-jet printers also accept larger paper, envelopes, labels and transparencies. Make sure you buy items designed specifically for use with ink-jet printers.

Ink-jet printers can use standard paper, but printing quality improves when you use more expensive, coated paper. Some ink-jet printers can also use special glossy paper to produce photographic quality images.

Color

Color ink-jet printers are very popular because they are less expensive than other types of color printers and still produce high-quality color images. A color ink-jet printer sprays cyan, magenta, yellow and black ink to create different colors on a page.

PRINTER

LASER PRINTER

A laser printer is a high-speed printer that is ideal for business and personal documents and for professional graphics work.

A laser printer works like a photocopier to produce high-quality images on a page.

Speed

Most laser printers produce images at a speed of 4 to 16 pages per minute (ppm).

All laser printers have a Central Processing Unit (CPU) that processes instructions and manages the flow of information in the printer. The CPU speed is a major factor in determining how fast a laser printer operates. The faster the CPU speed, the faster the printer will produce images.

Resolution

The resolution, or quality, of the images produced by a laser printer ranges from 600 to 2400 dots per inch (dpi).

Memory

Laser printers store pages in built-in memory before printing. A typical laser printer comes with 2 MB to 8 MB of memory.

Memory is important for laser printers that produce images at high resolutions, such as 2400 dpi. Memory is also important for laser printers that print on larger paper sizes and process complex print jobs.

Toner

Like photocopiers, laser printers use a fine powdered ink, called toner, which comes in a cartridge. When the toner runs out, you buy a new cartridge. Check the documentation that came with the printer to determine which type of cartridge the printer can use.

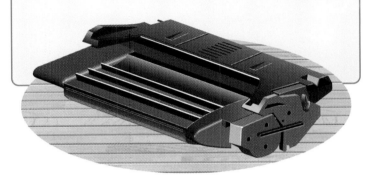

Paper

All laser printers can print on 8 1/2 by 11-inch paper, envelopes, labels and transparencies. For best results, check the printer's documentation to find the size, composition and weight of the paper the printer can use.

Color

You can buy laser printers that produce color images. A color laser printer is more expensive than a color ink jet printer, but it produces superior output.

OTHER TYPES OF PRINTERS

Dot-matrix Printer

A dot-matrix printer produces low-quality images. Inside a dot-matrix printer, a print head containing small, blunt pins strikes an inked ribbon. This is useful for printing on multipart forms that need an impact to print through multiple copies.

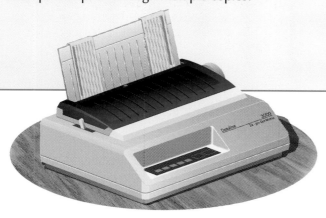

LED Printer

Light Emitting Diode (LED) printers are similar to laser printers, but produce images on a page by using several small lights. LED printers produce pages that are comparable in quality to laser printers, but LED printers are less expensive.

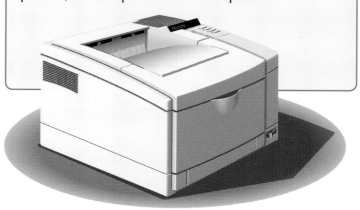

Color Photo Printer

A color photo printer is designed to produce photographic-quality images. This type of printer usually requires a special type of paper and may only accept paper in standard photographic sizes, such as 4x6.

Multifunction Printer

A multifunction printer can perform more than one task. This type of printer is often able to work as a fax machine, scanner and photocopier as well as a printer. Color multifunction printers are also available.

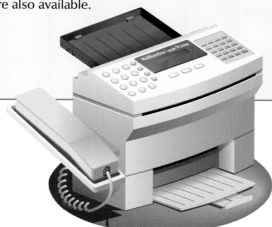

PRINT BUFFER AND SPOOLER

A computer can send data faster than a printer can accept and process the data. A print buffer or print spooler acts like a dam, holding the data and then releasing it at a speed the printer can handle.

Print Buffer

A print buffer is a section of memory in a printer that stores information waiting to print. When the buffer is full, the computer must wait before sending more data to the printer.

Print Spooler

A print spooler is a program on your computer that stores information waiting to print.

A print spooler can store more information than a print buffer and lets you continue using your computer without having to wait for a document to finish printing. Most operating systems set up a print spooler for each printer connected to the computer.

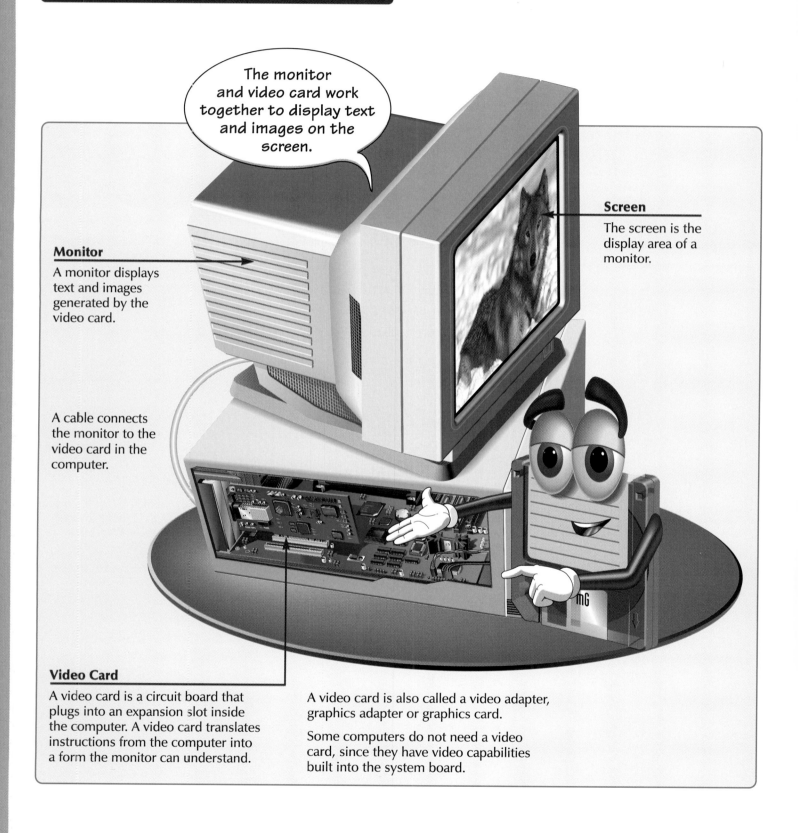

Monitor

A monitor displays text and images generated by the video card.

A cable connects the monitor to the video card in the computer.

Screen

The screen is the display area of a monitor.

Video Card

A video card is a circuit board that plugs into an expansion slot inside the computer. A video card translates instructions from the computer into a form the monitor can understand.

A video card is also called a video adapter, graphics adapter or graphics card.

Some computers do not need a video card, since they have video capabilities built into the system board.

CHOOSE A MONITOR

Size

The size of a monitor is measured diagonally across the screen. Common monitor sizes are 14, 15, 17 and 21 inches. Larger monitors are more expensive and are ideal for desktop publishing and working with graphics or large spreadsheets.

Manufacturers usually advertise the diagonal measurement of the picture tube inside the monitor, which is greater than the actual viewing area. Make sure you ask for the size of the viewing area.

Flat-panel

A flat-panel monitor uses Liquid Crystal Display (LCD), which is the same type of display found in most digital wristwatches. In the past, flat-panel screens were only used on portable computers, but now full-size flat-panel monitors are available for desktop computers.

Flat-panel monitors are more expensive than regular monitors, but are lighter, take up less desk space and use less electricity.

Dot Pitch

The dot pitch is the distance between pixels on a screen. A pixel is the smallest element on a screen. The dot pitch determines the sharpness of images on the screen and is measured in millimeters (mm).

The smaller the dot pitch, the crisper the images. Select a monitor with a dot pitch of 0.28 mm or less.

CHOOSE A MONITOR (CONTINUED)

Refresh Rate

The refresh rate determines the speed that a monitor redraws, or updates, images. The higher the refresh rate, the less flicker on the screen. This helps reduce eyestrain.

The refresh rate is measured in hertz (Hz) and tells you the number of times per second the monitor redraws the entire screen. A monitor with a refresh rate of 72 Hz or more is recommended.

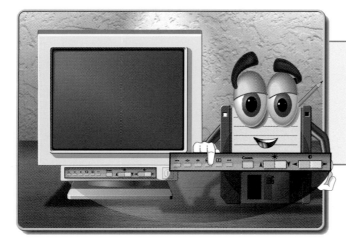

Controls

Monitors have controls to adjust the brightness, contrast and other features of the images displayed on the screen. You can find controls on the screen or on the monitor.

Tilt-and-swivel Base

A tilt-and-swivel base lets you adjust the angle of the screen. This lets you reduce the glare from overhead lighting and view the screen more comfortably.

Electromagnetic Radiation

Any device that uses electricity produces Electromagnetic Radiation (EMR). You can minimize the risk of EMR by buying a monitor that meets MPR II guidelines. The MPR II guidelines define acceptable levels of EMR.

The manual that came with your monitor may provide information about the ERM produced by the monitor and offer suggestions for protecting yourself from its potentially harmful effects.

Energy Star

The Environmental Protection Agency (EPA) developed an energy-saving guideline called ENERGY STAR to reduce wasted energy and the pollution it causes.

When you do not use an ENERGY STAR computer for a period of time, the monitor and computer enter an energy-saving sleep mode. You awaken the computer by moving the mouse or pressing a key on the keyboard.

MONITOR TIPS

Screen Saver

A screen saver is a moving picture or pattern that appears on the screen when you do not use a computer for a period of time.

Screen savers were originally designed to prevent screen burn, which occurs when an image appears in a fixed position for a period of time. Today's monitors are designed to prevent screen burn, but people still use screen savers for entertainment.

The Windows operating system provides several screen savers. You can also purchase screen savers at most computer stores.

Using a process called Webcasting, you can also use screen savers that display customized, up-to-the-minute information. This information is transferred to your computer over the Internet.

Glare Filter

A glare filter fits over the front of a monitor to reduce the amount of light reflected off the computer screen. This helps reduce eyestrain.

A glare filter may be able to block the radiation coming from the front of the monitor. Some glare filters make the screen difficult to read when viewed from an angle, which can help you keep your work private.

VIDEO CARD MEMORY

A video card has memory chips. These chips temporarily store information before sending it to the monitor.

Most computers require at least 2 MB of video card memory.

AGP

An Accelerated Graphics Port (AGP) video card uses an AGP bus to communicate directly with your computer's main memory. This allows you to quickly display complex images on your monitor.

AGP is specially designed to meet the high demands of displaying 3D images.

3D GRAPHICS ACCELERATOR CARD

A 3D graphics accelerator card has a specialized chip, called a Graphics Processing Unit (GPU), that is optimized to produce 3D graphics. A GPU allows a card to display information on the screen without using your computer's processor.

This type of video card is required for playing some graphic intensive games that display 3D images.

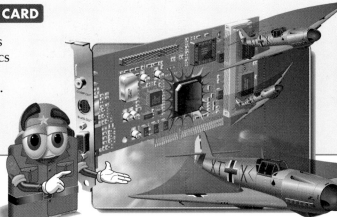

RESOLUTION

Resolution is measured by the number of horizontal and vertical pixels. A pixel is the smallest element on the screen. Pixel is short for picture element.

Most monitors can detect which resolution and refresh rate the video card is using and then automatically switch to the appropriate settings.

Resolution determines the amount of information a monitor can display.

Most monitors also let you adjust the resolution to suit your needs. To be able to change the resolution of a monitor, the video card must be able to use the same resolution.

| 640 x 480 | 800 x 600 | 1,024 x 768 | 1,280 x 1,024 | 1,600 x 1,280 |

  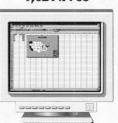 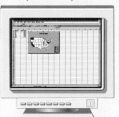 

Lower resolutions display larger images so you can see information more clearly.

Higher resolutions display smaller images so you can display more information at once.

COLOR DEPTH

The video card you use determines the number of colors a monitor can display. More colors result in more realistic images.

16 Colors (4-bit color)

Choppy-looking images.

256 Colors (8-bit color)

Suitable for most home, business and game applications.

65,536 Colors (16-bit color)

Useful for video and desktop publishing applications. Unless you are a trained professional, it is difficult to distinguish between 16-bit and 24-bit color.

16,777,216 Colors (24-bit color)

Useful for photographic work. This setting is also called true color because it displays more colors than the human eye can distinguish.

16,777,216 Colors (32-bit color)

Useful for graphic intensive games. This setting works more efficiently and faster than 24-bit color.

MODEM

A modem lets computers exchange information through telephone lines.

A modem translates computer information into a form that can transmit over phone lines. The receiving modem translates the information it receives into a form the computer can understand.

PHONE LINE

You can use the same phone line for telephone and modem calls, but you will not be able to use the telephone and the modem at the same time. If your telephone and modem share the same line, make sure you turn off the call waiting feature when using your modem, since this feature could disrupt the modem connection.

ACCESS INFORMATION

You can use a modem to connect to the Internet so you can access information and meet people with similar interests.

When traveling or at home, you can use a modem to access information stored on the network at work. You can send and receive electronic mail (e-mail) and work with office files.

SEND AND RECEIVE FAXES

Most modems can send and receive faxes. With a fax modem, you can create a document on your computer and then fax the document to another computer or fax machine.

VOICE CAPABILITIES

Some modems have voice capabilities that allow you to use the modem to send and receive voice telephone calls. This lets you use the modem as a hands-free telephone. You may also be able to use a modem with voice capabilities as an answering machine for voice telephone messages.

TYPES OF MODEMS

Internal Modem

An internal modem is a circuit board that plugs into an expansion slot inside a computer. An internal modem is generally less expensive than an external modem, but is more difficult to set up.

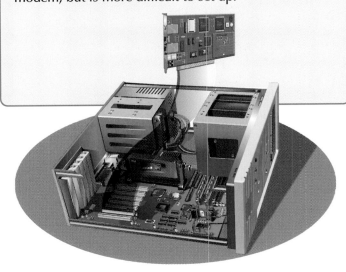

External Modem

An external modem is a small box that connects to the back of a computer. An external modem takes up room on your desk, but can be used with more than one computer.

MODEM

MODEM SPEED

The speed of a modem determines how fast it can send and receive information through telephone lines.

Modem speed is measured in bits per second (bps). You should buy a modem with a speed of 56,000 bps.

Modem speed is also measured in kilobits per second (Kbps). For example, a 56,000 bps modem is also referred to as a 56 Kbps modem.

Buy the fastest modem you can afford. Faster modems transfer information more quickly. This will save you time and reduce online service charges and long distance charges.

Line Quality

The speed at which information transfers depends on the quality of the phone line. For example, a modem with a speed of 56 Kbps may not reach that speed if the phone line quality is poor.

Modem Standards

Modem standards ensure that modems made by different manufacturers can communicate with each other. V.90 is the current standard for 56 Kbps modems, though a new V.92 standard has been proposed. A V.90 modem can receive data at a speed of 56 Kbps but can only send data at a speed of 33.6 Kbps.

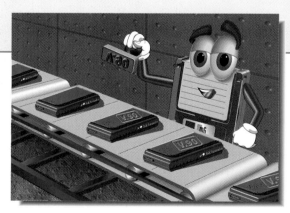

HOW MODEMS COMMUNICATE

Communications Program

A modem needs a communications program to manage the transmission of information with another modem. This type of program usually comes packaged with a modem.

Handshake

When your modem first contacts another modem, you may hear a series of squeals and signals. This is called a handshake. Just as two people shake hands to greet each other, modems perform a handshake to establish how they will exchange information.

Online

You are online when your modem has successfully connected to another modem. This means the modems are ready to exchange information. When your modem is not connected to another modem, you are offline.

DATA COMPRESSION

A modem can compress, or squeeze together, data sent to another modem to speed the transfer of data. The speed of data transfer depends on the type of file being sent. For example, a text file will compress significantly more than an image file.

When the information reaches its intended destination, the receiving modem decompresses the information.

A modem uses error control to ensure that information reliably reaches its destination.

There are several types of high-speed connections that you can use to connect to the Internet instead of using a modem.

High-speed connections are sometimes referred to as broadband connections.

ADVANTAGES OF HIGH-SPEED CONNECTIONS

Frees up Telephone Line

Unlike a modem, a high-speed connection does not tie up your telephone line while you are on the Internet. This allows you to make telephone calls or use a fax machine while you are connected to the Internet.

24-Hour Connection

A high-speed connection allows you to be connected to the Internet 24-hours a day. This saves you from having to dial-in to your Internet service provider each time you want to connect to the Internet. This is useful when you want to continuously monitor information, such as financial news.

Fast Access

Using a high-speed connection allows you to quickly access information of interest on the Internet. For example, sound and video transfer to your computer faster, so you can watch live video on the Internet more easily.

TYPES OF HIGH-SPEED CONNECTIONS

ISDN

An Integrated Services Digital Network (ISDN) line is a digital phone line offered by telephone companies in most cities. An ISDN line can transfer information at speeds from 56 Kbps to 128 Kbps.

Cable Modem

A cable modem allows you to connect to the Internet with the same type of cable that attaches to a television set. A cable modem can transfer information at a speed of up to 4,000 Kbps. You can contact your local cable company to determine if they offer cable Internet service.

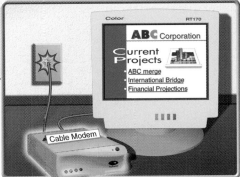

DSL

Digital Subscriber Line (DSL) is a high-speed digital phone line service offered by telephone companies in most cities. DSL can transfer information at speeds from 1,000 Kbps to 6,000 Kbps.

Emerging Technologies

Companies are constantly working on ways to send more information over the Internet at faster speeds. Some technologies that are currently emerging include using satellites and electric power lines to connect to the Internet and transfer information.

SOUND CARD

A sound card is a circuit board that lets a computer play and record high-quality sound.

A sound card is also called a sound board or audio card.

A sound card plugs into an expansion slot in a computer. Some computers do not need a sound card, since they have sound capabilities built into the system board.

Speakers

Speakers allow you to hear the sound generated by a sound card. Most computers come equipped with low-quality speakers.

You may want to upgrade to higher quality speakers if you use your computer to play games or listen to music.

SOUND CARD APPLICATIONS

Games and Multimedia Presentations

A sound card lets you hear music, speech and sound effects during games and multimedia presentations.

Record Sounds

You can use a sound card to record music, speech and sound effects. You can then add the sounds to documents and presentations. You can also use a sound card to compose music on your computer.

SOUND CARD CONNECTIONS

The edge of your sound card may look different from the sound card shown here.

You can see the edge of a sound card at the back of a computer. A sound card has a port and several jacks where you can plug in external devices.

Game Port

This port lets you connect a joystick or a MIDI device such as a music keyboard.

Speaker Jack

This jack lets you connect speakers or headphones to hear sound generated by a sound card.

GAMEPORT | SPK OUT | LINE OUT | MIC IN | LINE IN

Line Out Jack

This jack lets you connect an amplifier to play sound through your home stereo.

Microphone Jack

This jack lets you connect a microphone to record speech and other sounds.

Line In Jack

This jack lets you connect a cassette or CD player to play music.

SOUND CARD

There are several factors to consider when choosing a sound card.

CHOOSE A SOUND CARD

Sampling Rate

The sampling rate of a sound card determines the quality of the sound produced.

For good sound quality, buy a sound card with a sampling rate of at least 44.1 KHz.

If possible, listen to the sounds produced by various sound cards before making your purchase.

Full-duplex

A full-duplex sound card lets you talk and listen at the same time. When using a computer to have a conversation over the Internet, a full-duplex sound card lets people talk at the same time. With a half-duplex sound card, people must take turns talking.

3-D Sound

A sound card that offers 3-D sound capabilities produces sound that seems to come from several directions. 3-D sound cards are often used to enhance the sounds in computer games.

MIDI SUPPORT

Musical Instrument Digital Interface (MIDI) is a set of instructions that allow computers and musical devices to exchange data. This lets you connect a musical instrument, such as a synthesizer, to a computer to play, record and edit music. Many musicians use MIDI to compose music on a computer.

A sound card that supports MIDI also ensures that a computer can generate the sounds in games, multimedia CD-ROMs and presentation packages.

> There are two ways a sound card can produce MIDI sound.

Wavetable Synthesis

Wavetable synthesis uses actual recordings of musical instruments and speech to produce MIDI sound. This results in rich, realistic sound. Wavetable synthesis is now available on most sound cards.

FM Synthesis

FM synthesis is an older method of producing MIDI sound. This method uses mathematical formulas to imitate the sounds of musical instruments and speech, resulting in less realistic sound. FM synthesis is available on some low-range quality sound cards.

A TV tuner card allows you to watch television programs on your computer.

TV tuner cards combine computer and television technology. This combination, or convergence, of technologies is creating an exciting new form of entertainment and communication.

A TV tuner card is a circuit board that plugs into an expansion slot in a computer.

Video Card

TV tuner cards require a video card to operate. Some TV tuner cards connect to the video card in your computer, but many TV tuner cards have a built-in video card.

TV TUNER CARD FEATURES

Resize

TV tuner cards can display a television program using the entire display area of a monitor or using a window that you can easily resize to suit your needs. This is useful if you want to watch a television program while performing other tasks on your computer.

Closed Captioning

Most TV tuner cards can help you find television programs of interest by scanning the closed captioning text of a television channel for a keyword you specify. When the keyword appears, the TV tuner card displays the television program on your monitor. Most TV tuner cards also allow you to save the closed captioning text from a television program as a file on your hard drive.

Intercast Technology

Some television channels use Intercast technology to broadcast additional information with their programs. This allows you to watch a television program and view text and images related to the program at the same time.

For example, when you watch a car race, you can also view information such as the average speed of a driver. Most TV tuner cards support Intercast technology.

Video Capture

Most TV tuner cards allow you to save still images and full-motion video clips from a television program as a file on your hard drive. You can then use these images and video clips in documents, e-mail messages or presentations.

SCANNER

A scanner is a device that reads images and text into a computer.

SCAN IMAGES

You can scan images such as photographs, drawings and logos into a computer. You can then use the images in documents, such as reports or newsletters.

Most scanners come with image editing software, which lets you change the appearance of a scanned image.

SCAN TEXT

You can scan text to quickly enter documents into a computer. This lets you scan interesting paper documents and e-mail them to friends or colleagues. You can also scan documents to store them on your computer for quick access.

Most scanners come with Optical Character Recognition (OCR) software. This software places scanned text into a document that can be edited in a word processor.

TYPES OF SCANNERS

Flatbed Scanner

A flatbed scanner can scan single sheets of paper and pages from a book. Most flatbed scanners can scan documents that measure 8½ by 11 inches. Some flatbed scanners can scan larger documents.

Sheet-fed Scanner

A sheet-fed scanner can scan only single sheets of paper. If you want to scan a page from a book, you have to tear out the page. Sheet-fed scanners are less expensive and more compact than flatbed scanners, but produce lower quality images.

Handheld Scanner

A handheld scanner usually has a scanning width of approximately four inches and is useful for copying small images such as signatures, logos and small photographs.

Smaller handheld scanners that resemble highlighter pens are also available. These scanners are useful for scanning lines of text.

SCANNER

COLOR DEPTH

The color depth of a scanner is measured in bits and indicates the number of colors the scanner can detect. The more colors the scanner can detect, the higher the quality of the scan. Current scanners commonly have a 36-bit color depth.

SCANNING MODE

When scanning an image, you can choose the scanning mode. The scanning mode you choose will affect the quality of the scan and the amount of space the scanned image takes up on your computer.

Line Art

The line art mode scans an image using black and white, creating a scanned image with a small file size.

Grayscale

The grayscale mode scans an image using black, white and shades of gray. This creates an image with a larger file size than the line art mode.

Color

The color mode scans an image using shades of red, blue and green, resulting in a scanned image with a larger file size.

**RESOLUTION**

The resolution of a scanner determines the amount of detail the scanner can detect. Scanner resolution is measured in dots per inch (dpi). Common scanner resolutions range from 600 dpi to 2400 dpi.

Resolution can also be expressed with two numbers (example: 600 x 1200 dpi). These numbers describe the number of dots a scanner can detect across and down one square inch.

Choose the Resolution

Scanning an image at a high resolution results in a clearer, more detailed image, but requires more scanning time and storage space.

You usually do not need to scan an image at a higher resolution than a printer can produce or a monitor can display.

20 dpi

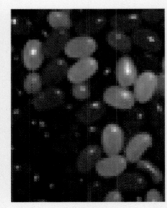
72 dpi

300 dpi

If you plan to print an image on a 300 dpi printer, you do not need to scan at a resolution higher than 300 dpi. Monitors have a maximum resolution of 72 dpi. If you plan to display an image on a monitor or on the Internet, you do not need to scan at a resolution higher than 72 dpi.

DIGITAL CAMERA

A digital camera lets you take photos that you can use on your computer.

Most digital cameras come with image editing software that allows you to view and edit the photos you take.

WORK WITH PHOTOS

You can transfer photos from a digital camera to a computer. This lets you use the photos in documents, on the World Wide Web or in e-mail messages.

If you want prints of the photos you take, you can have a company such as Kodak develop the photos for a fee. You can also buy a color photo printer to print your own photos.

FEATURES

Most digital cameras come with a color Liquid Crystal Display (LCD) screen, which is the same type of display found in notebook computers. You can use the LCD screen to preview your shots and view photos you have taken.

Most digital cameras include a built-in flash. You may also want to look for other features such as a zoom lens and the ability to record short videos.

MEGAPIXELS

The quality of photos a digital camera can produce depends on the detail the camera can detect. This detail, or resolution, is measured in megapixels. One megapixel is equivalent to a resolution of approximately 1000 x 1000 pixels. The higher the number of megapixels a camera can detect, the clearer and more detailed the photos. There are currently 1, 2 and 3-megapixel digital cameras available.

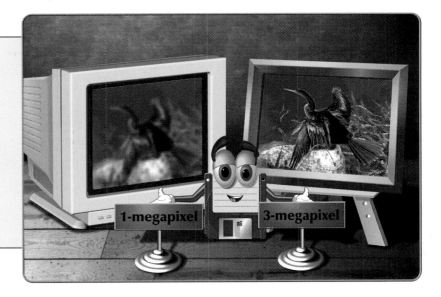

MEMORY

Digital cameras store photos in memory until you transfer the photos to your computer. Digital cameras can have removable or built-in memory.

Removable

Most digital cameras with removable memory store photos on a memory card. Some digital cameras store photos on a regular floppy disk that fits inside the camera. Once a memory card or floppy disk is full, you can replace the card or disk in the camera to continue storing photos.

Built-in

Once the memory in a digital camera with built-in memory is full, you must transfer the photos to your computer. You can then store new photos in the camera's memory.

DIGITAL VIDEO CAMERA

A digital video camera is a video camera that records video in a format that can be saved on a computer.

RESOLUTION

Digital video cameras use a device called a Charged Coupling Device (CCD) to capture video. The quality of video a digital video camera can produce depends on the amount of detail the CCD can detect. This detail, or resolution, is measured in pixels. The higher the number of pixels, the clearer and more detailed the video. Most digital video cameras have CCDs with a resolution between 250,000 and 700,000 pixels.

VIDEO EDITING SOFTWARE

You can use video editing software to edit videos saved on your computer. Some operating systems come with video editing software. For example, the Windows Me operating system includes Windows Movie Maker. You can also find video editing software at computer stores.

WEB CAMERA

A Web camera is a device that allows you to send live video over the Internet.

You can also use a Web camera to record videos that you can save on your computer.

VIDEOCONFERENCING

Web cameras are often used for videoconferencing. Videoconferencing allows you to have face-to-face conversations with people on the Internet or other networks.

Your computer must have a sound card, speakers and a microphone to transmit and receive sound during a videoconference.

RESOLUTION AND SPEED

The resolution and speed of a Web camera determine the quality of images it can produce. Web cameras often offer several resolutions and speeds you can choose from. Higher resolutions produce clearer and more detailed video, though the video transfers more slowly. A slow speed can cause a video to appear choppy.

Web cameras can commonly transfer video at a speed of 15 frames per second and a resolution of 640 x 480 pixels or a speed of 30 frames per second at a resolution of 352 x 288 pixels.

15 frames/s
640 x 480

30 frames/s
352 x 288

A portable MP3 player is a device that stores MP3 music files so you can listen to the music when you are away from your computer.

MP3 is a sound format used to transfer CD-quality music over the Internet. MP3 stands for Motion Picture Experts Group Audio Layer 3. The MP3 format compresses sound files so they take up small amounts of disk space.

Popular portable MP3 players include S3's Rio and Creative Labs' Nomad Jukebox.

Most portable MP3 players are solid-state devices, which means they have no moving parts. This allows you to listen to music while you are jogging or exercising without worrying about the music skipping.

You can connect a portable MP3 player to your computer to transfer MP3 files from the computer to the player. Once you have transferred files to the MP3 player, you can disconnect the player from the computer.

MEMORY

Many portable MP3 players use flash memory, which is a type of memory that can be quickly erased and re-recorded. Flash memory can be built-in memory or a removable memory card that fits inside the MP3 player. MP3 players with flash memory commonly offer 64 MB of memory, which allows you to store up to an hour of high quality music.

Some portable MP3 players have built-in hard drives, providing more storage space. For example, Creative Labs' Nomad Jukebox has a 6 GB hard drive that can store up to 100 hours of music.

OBTAIN MP3 FILES

There are many companies on the Web, such as EMusic.com and MP3.com, that allow you to download, or copy, individual songs or entire CDs in the MP3 format to your computer. Some companies offer the music for free and some require you to purchase the music.

You can also obtain an MP3 encoder program, such as the MusicMatch Jukebox program, that allows you to convert the songs on a CD to the MP3 format.

USB

A Universal Serial Bus (USB) port is a connector that can support up to 127 devices, such as a printer, mouse and external modem. Most new computers come with two USB ports. If your computer does not have a USB port, you can purchase a USB expansion card to add a USB port to the computer.

Speed

The current version of USB can transfer information at a speed of up to 12 megabits per second (Mbps). A new version of USB, called USB 2.0 or USB2, is currently in production. USB 2.0 will be able to transfer information at a speed of up to 480 Mbps.

FIREWIRE

A FireWire port is a connector that can support up to 63 devices. Some new computers come with two or more FireWire ports. If your computer does not have a FireWire port, you can purchase a FireWire expansion card. FireWire is also known as IEEE 1394 or i.LINK.

Speed

A FireWire port can transfer information at a speed of up to 400 Mbps. This makes a FireWire port useful for connecting high-speed devices such as digital video cameras and external hard drives.

CONNECT DEVICES

USB and FireWire ports allow you to easily connect new devices to your computer. When you plug a device into a USB or FireWire port, your computer can automatically detect and set up the device for you.

The type of port you use will depend on the device you want to connect. A device must be FireWire-compatible to connect to a FireWire port. Similarly, only USB-compatible devices can connect to a USB port. You can check a device's documentation to determine the type of port the device uses.

CHAPTER 3

PROCESSING

Wondering how a computer operates and processes information? Find out how in this chapter.

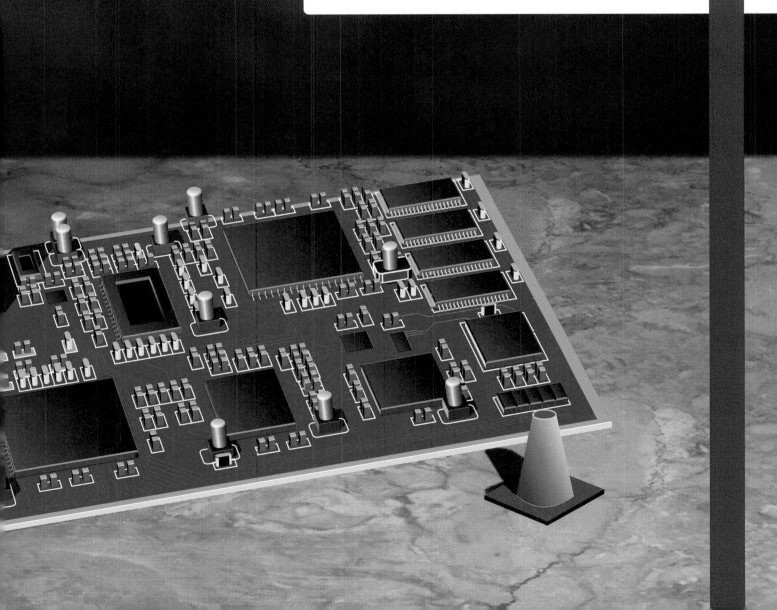

MEMORY

Memory, also called Random Access Memory (RAM), temporarily stores data inside a computer.

Memory works like a blackboard that is constantly overwritten with new data. The data stored in memory disappears when you turn off the computer.

MEMORY SIZE

The amount of memory determines the number of programs a computer can run at once and how fast programs will operate.

Memory is measured in megabytes (MB). You should buy a computer with at least 64 MB of memory.

You can improve the performance of a computer by adding more memory. The capabilities of your system board may limit the amount of memory you can add.

ACCESS SPEED

The speed at which information is stored and accessed in memory is called access speed. Access speed is usually measured in megahertz (MHz). When adding memory to your computer, make sure the access speed of the memory is compatible with the speed of the system board. Most system boards can support memory with an access speed of 100 MHz.

MEMORY CHIPS

Dynamic RAM (DRAM) is a type of memory chip that makes up the main memory in many computer systems.

Synchronous DRAM (SDRAM) is a faster type of memory chip found in most new computer systems. Many computers can use both DRAM and SDRAM memory chips.

Rambus DRAM (RDRAM) is a new type of memory chip often found in high-performance computers.

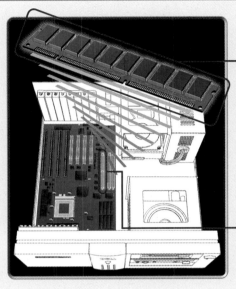

Memory Module

A memory module is a circuit board that holds memory chips. A Single In-line Memory Module (SIMM) holds up to nine memory chips. New computers also accept Dual In-line Memory Modules (DIMMs), which can hold up to 18 memory chips. You can add more memory to a computer by inserting additional memory modules.

Memory Module Socket

A memory module socket is a socket on the system board where you plug in a memory module.

VIRTUAL MEMORY

If you have limited memory or you have many programs open, your computer may need to use part of the hard drive to simulate more memory.

This simulated memory is called virtual memory and allows the computer to continue operating, but at a much slower speed.

ROM

Unlike RAM, Read-Only Memory (ROM) is permanent and cannot be changed. ROM stores instructions that help prepare the computer for use each time you turn on the computer.

The Central Processing Unit (CPU) is the main chip in a computer.

The CPU processes instructions, performs calculations and manages the flow of information through a computer system. The CPU performs millions of calculations every second.

The CPU is also called the microprocessor or processor.

CPU COMPLEXITY

Imagine a road map of the United States printed on a fingernail and you can imagine the complexity of a CPU. The elements in a CPU can be as small as 0.18 microns wide. By comparison, a human hair is approximately 100 microns wide.

The manufacturing plants that produce CPUs must be many times cleaner than hospital operating rooms. Ultra-sensitive dust filtering systems are needed to eliminate particles that could damage the CPUs during production.

There are several factors that determine the performance of a CPU.

CHOOSE A CPU

Manufacturer

The most popular CPUs for personal computers are made by Intel. Other popular CPU manufacturers include AMD and VIA Technologies.

Generation

Each new generation of CPU is more powerful than the one before. Newer CPUs can process more instructions at a time. For example, a newer generation CPU such as the Intel Pentium 4 is more powerful than an older CPU such as the Intel Pentium III.

Speed

Each type of CPU is available in several speeds. The CPU speed is a major factor in determining how fast a computer operates. The faster the speed, the faster the computer operates.

The speed of a CPU is commonly measured in megahertz (MHz), or millions of cycles per second. New, faster CPUs are now measured in gigahertz (GHz), or billions of cycles per second.

TYPES OF CPUs

Intel Pentium Processor

Pentium is a popular type of CPU manufactured by Intel. There are several generations of Intel Pentium CPUs, including Pentium, Pentium II, Pentium III and Pentium 4. Intel Pentium 4 is the most recent generation, with a processing speed of over 1 GHz.

Intel Pentium III CPUs are still found in many new computers, while the older Pentium II and Pentium generations are now less common. Intel Pentium III CPUs are available with speeds from 450 MHz to 1.13 GHz.

Intel Celeron Processor

Intel's Celeron CPU is an inexpensive CPU designed to meet the needs and budgets of most home computer users. Intel Celeron CPUs are similar to Intel Pentium II CPUs, but have less built-in memory. Intel Celeron CPUs are available with speeds from 500 to 700 MHz.

AMD Athlon Processor

The AMD Athlon CPU is a high-performance processor manufactured by AMD. This CPU is suitable for businesses and home computer users who want a powerful processor.

AMD Athlon CPUs are available with speeds from 800 MHz to 1.1 GHz.

AMD Duron Processor

AMD manufactures the AMD Duron CPU, which is an inexpensive CPU that meets the needs of most home computer users. AMD Duron CPUs offer relatively high speeds at a low cost.

AMD Duron CPUs are available with speeds of 650, 700 and 750 MHz.

VIA Cyrix Processor

Cyrix is a type of CPU manufactured by VIA Technologies. VIA Cyrix CPUs are available in two generations—VIA Cyrix MII and VIA Cyrix III. These CPUs are designed for businesses and home computer users who want an inexpensive CPU with good quality processing capabilities.

The VIA Cyrix MII is available with speeds from 300 to 433 MHz. The VIA Cyrix III is available with speeds from 500 to 600 MHz.

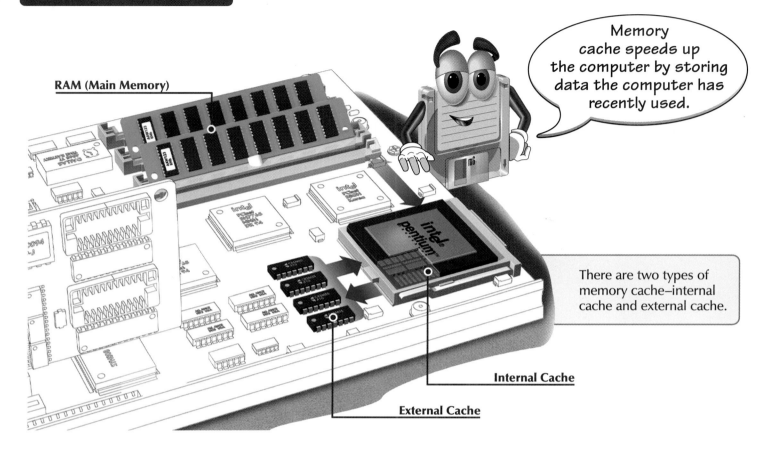

RAM (Main Memory)

Memory cache speeds up the computer by storing data the computer has recently used.

There are two types of memory cache—internal cache and external cache.

Internal Cache

External Cache

INTERNAL CACHE

When a computer needs data, the computer first looks in the internal cache. Internal cache is on the CPU chip and provides the fastest way for the computer to get data. Internal cache is also called L1 or primary cache.

EXTERNAL CACHE

If the computer cannot find the data it needs in the internal cache, the computer looks in the external cache. External cache is usually on the system board and consists of Static RAM (SRAM) chips.

Accessing external cache is generally slower than internal cache, but is much faster than retrieving data from RAM. In some computers, the external cache is built into the CPU chip, which makes accessing the cache much faster.

RAM

If the computer cannot find the data it needs in the internal or external cache, the computer must get the data from the slower main memory, called RAM.

Each time the computer requests data from RAM, the computer places a copy of the data in the memory cache. This process constantly updates the memory cache so it always contains the most recently used data.

USING MEMORY CACHE

Using memory cache is similar to working with documents in your office. When you need information, you look for information in a specific order. Each step along the way takes up more of your valuable time.

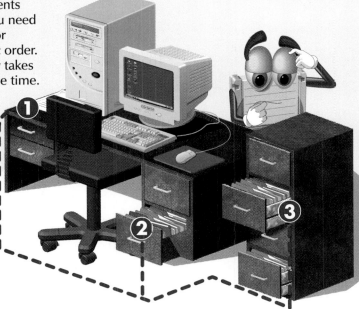

❶ Look through documents on your desk (internal cache).

❷ Look through documents in your desk drawer (external cache).

❸ Look through documents in your filing cabinet (RAM).

Working without memory cache would be similar to looking through the filing cabinet each time you need a document.

The bus is the electronic pathway that carries information between devices in a computer.

BUS WIDTH

The bus width is similar to the number of lanes on a highway. The greater the width, the more data can flow along the bus at a time. Bus width is measured in bits. Eight bits equals one character.

BUS SPEED

The bus speed is similar to the speed limit on a highway. The higher the speed, the faster data travels along the bus. Bus speed is measured in megahertz (MHz), or millions of cycles per second.

BUS TYPES

ISA Bus

The Industry Standard Architecture (ISA) bus is the slowest and oldest type of bus. This bus is often used for transferring information to and from a slow device, such as a modem. The ISA bus has a width of 16 bits and a speed of 8 MHz.

The ISA bus is found in Pentium and Pentium II computers.

PCI Bus

The Peripheral Component Interconnect (PCI) bus is a sophisticated type of bus found in new computers. This bus can handle many high-speed devices. The PCI bus can have a width of 32 or 64 bits and a speed of up to 66 MHz.

The PCI bus supports Plug and Play, which lets you add new devices to a computer without complex installation procedures.

The PCI bus is found in Pentium II, Pentium III and Pentium 4 computers.

AGP Bus

An Accelerated Graphics Port (AGP) bus is specifically designed to carry complex graphics data between an AGP video card and your computer's main memory. The AGP bus has a width of 32 bits and a speed of 66 MHz.

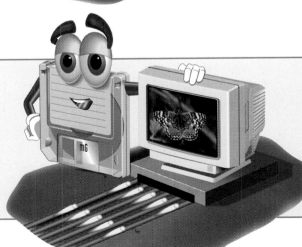

The AGP bus is found in Pentium II, Pentium III and Pentium 4 computers.

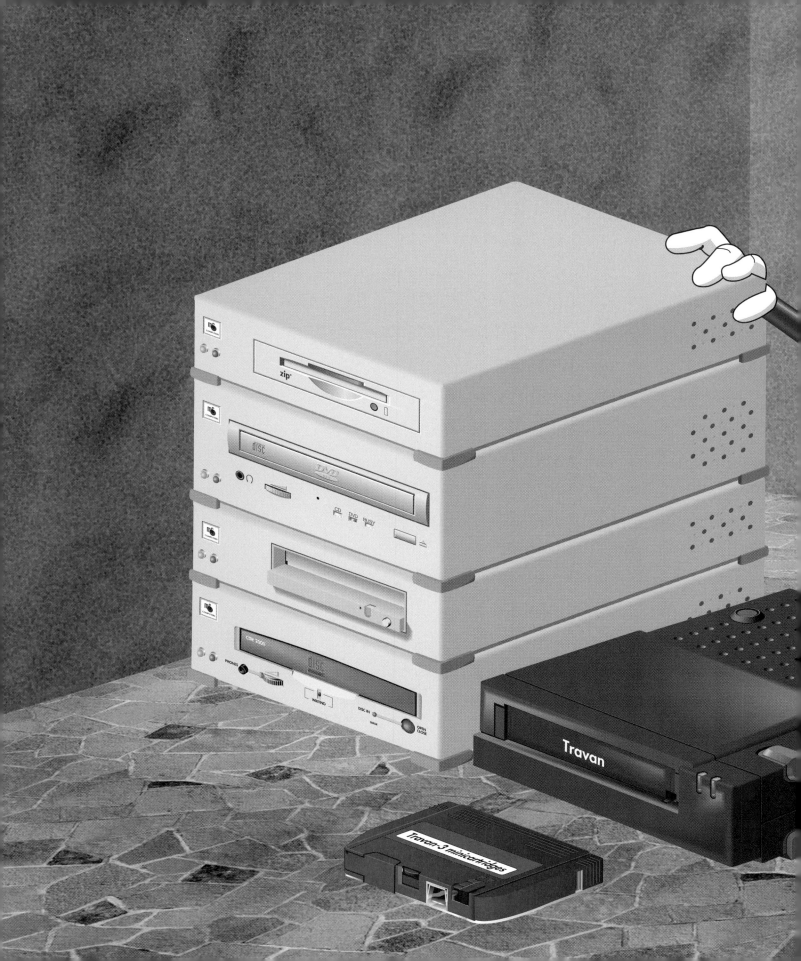

CHAPTER 4

STORAGE DEVICES

What is a hard drive? What does a CD-RW drive do? Learn about storage devices in this chapter.

HARD DRIVE

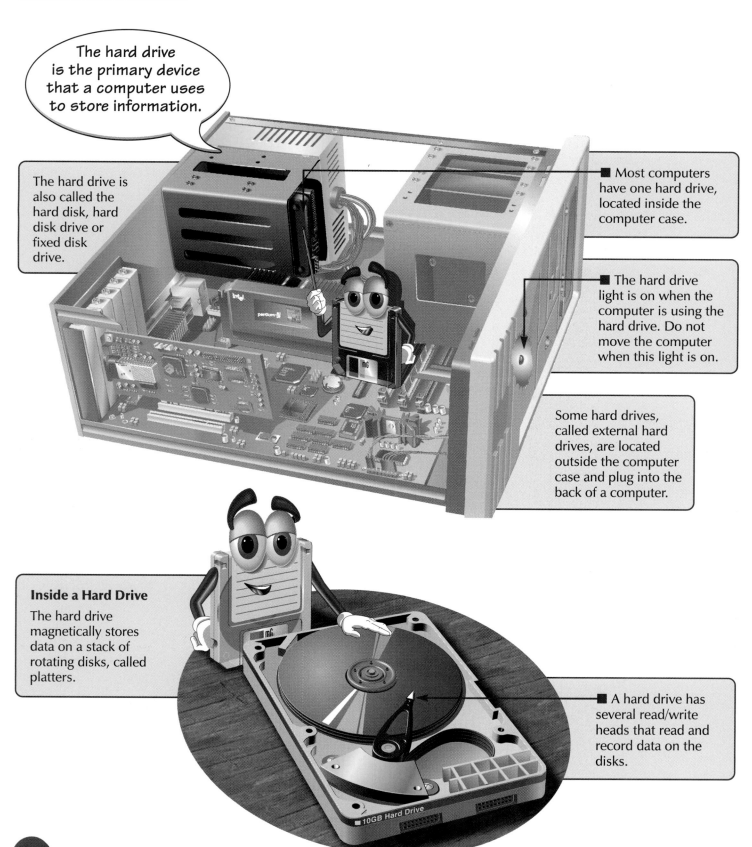

The hard drive is the primary device that a computer uses to store information.

The hard drive is also called the hard disk, hard disk drive or fixed disk drive.

■ Most computers have one hard drive, located inside the computer case.

■ The hard drive light is on when the computer is using the hard drive. Do not move the computer when this light is on.

Some hard drives, called external hard drives, are located outside the computer case and plug into the back of a computer.

Inside a Hard Drive

The hard drive magnetically stores data on a stack of rotating disks, called platters.

■ A hard drive has several read/write heads that read and record data on the disks.

■ 10GB Hard Drive

HARD DRIVE CONTENTS

Program Files

A hard drive stores your operating system and programs. When you buy a new program, you must install, or copy, the program files to your hard drive before you can use the program.

Programs come on a CD-ROM disc, DVD-ROM disc or several floppy disks.

Data Files

A hard drive stores your data files, such as documents, spreadsheets and images.

STORE FILES

Save Files

When you are creating a document, the computer stores the document in temporary memory. If you want to store a document for future use, you can save the document to the hard drive. If you do not save the document, the document will be lost when there is a power failure or you turn off the computer.

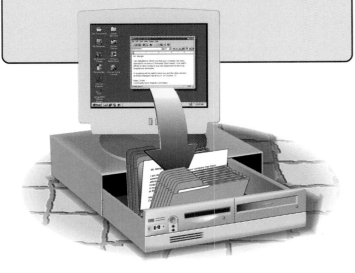

File System

The file system determines how information is stored on a hard drive. The file system your computer uses depends on the operating system you are using and how the computer is set up. Common file systems include FAT, FAT32 and NTFS.

HARD DRIVE

CHOOSE A HARD DRIVE

Capacity

The amount of information a hard drive can store is measured in bytes.

A hard drive with a capacity of 5 to 10 GB will suit most home and business users.

Purchase the largest hard drive you can afford. New programs and data will quickly fill a hard drive. For example, Microsoft Office requires about 250 MB of hard drive space. The Windows Me operating system requires about 300 MB.

Speed

The speed at which the platters in the hard drive spin is measured in Revolutions Per Minute (RPM). The higher the RPM, the faster the hard drive can find and record data on the platters.

The speed at which a hard drive finds data is referred to as the average access time. Average access time is measured in milliseconds (ms). One millisecond equals 1/1000 of a second. Most hard drives have an average access time of 8 to 15 ms. The lower the average access time, the faster the hard drive.

CONNECTION TYPE

EIDE

Enhanced Integrated Drive Electronics (EIDE) is a fast way to connect a hard drive and other devices to a computer. Most computers come with an EIDE connection. EIDE is often referred to as IDE.

EIDE can support a total of four devices, including hard drives, CD-ROM drives, DVD-ROM drives and tape drives.

Ultra Direct Memory Access (UDMA) is an enhancement to EIDE that increases the speed at which data transfers over an EIDE connection.

SCSI

Small Computer System Interface (SCSI, pronounced "scuzzy") is the fastest, most flexible, but most expensive way to connect a hard drive and other devices to a computer.

The most common type of SCSI can connect up to seven devices, including removable drives, CD-ROM drives, DVD-ROM drives, tape drives and scanners. There are also other types of SCSI available that transmit data faster and connect more devices.

DISK CACHE

The disk cache speeds up the computer by storing data the computer has recently used.

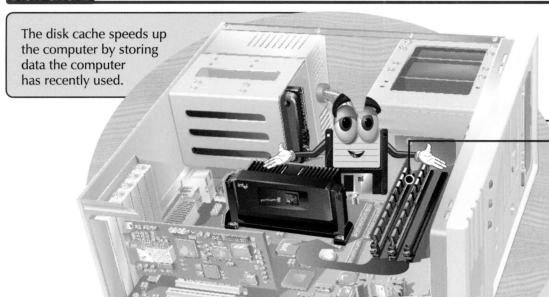

■ The disk cache is an area of memory where the computer stores recently used data.

When the computer needs data, the computer first looks in the disk cache. The disk cache can supply data thousands of times faster than the hard drive.

If the computer cannot find the data it needs in the disk cache, the computer looks on the hard drive.

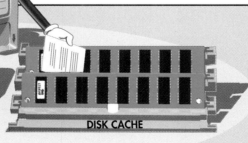

HARD DRIVE

DISK CACHE

Each time the computer requests data from the hard drive, the computer places a copy of the data in the disk cache. This process constantly updates the disk cache so it always contains the most recently used data.

PROTECT A HARD DRIVE

Virus

A virus is a program that disrupts the normal operation of a computer. A virus can cause a variety of problems, such as the appearance of annoying messages on the screen or the destruction of information on the hard drive.

Files you receive on a floppy disk or from the Internet may contain viruses. You should use a virus scanner program to regularly check your computer for viruses.

Back Up Data

You should copy the files stored on your hard drive to removable disks or tape cartridges. This provides extra copies in case the original files are lost or damaged due to viruses or computer failure.

You do not need to back up the programs stored on your computer if you have the original program disc or disks. If a program on your hard drive is lost or damaged, you can use the original disc or disks to re-install the program at any time.

OPTIMIZE A HARD DRIVE

Defragment a Drive

A fragmented hard drive stores parts of a file in many different locations. To retrieve a file, the computer must search many areas of the drive.

You can use a defragmentation program to place all parts of a file in one location. This reduces the time the hard drive spends locating the file.

Defragmenting your hard drive once a month can improve the performance of the computer. Most operating systems include a defragmentation program

Repair a Drive

You can improve the performance of a computer by using a disk repair program to search for and repair disk errors. You should check a hard drive for errors at least once a month.

Most operating systems include a disk repair program.

CREATE MORE DISK SPACE

Archive Information

Store old or rarely used files on a tape cartridge or a removable disk. You can then remove the files from your computer to provide more storage space.

Disk Cleanup

You can use a disk cleanup program to find and remove files that are no longer needed on your computer, such as temporary files. Removing unneeded files will free up space on a hard drive.

Many operating systems include a disk cleanup program.

Data Compression

You can compress, or squeeze together, the files stored on a hard drive. This can double the amount of information the drive can store.

You should only compress a hard drive if it is running out of space to store new information and you have tried all other ways of increasing the available storage space.

Most operating systems include a disk compression program.

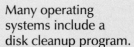

A floppy drive stores and retrieves information on floppy disks.

Most computers have a floppy drive, called drive A.

FLOPPY DISK

A floppy drive stores information on floppy disks, or diskettes. A floppy disk is a removable device that magnetically stores data.

Marketing Strategy

MicroFLOPPY
Double Sided
1.44 MB

Floppy disks are commonly used for transferring data from one computer to another. This lets you give data to friends and colleagues.

Floppy drives use 3.5 inch floppy disks. Inside a 3.5 inch floppy disk is a thin, flexible, plastic disk that magnetically records information. The word floppy refers to this flexible disk.

INSERT A FLOPPY DISK

Push the floppy disk gently into the drive, label side up. Most drives make a "click" sound when you have fully inserted the disk.

■ This light is on when the computer is using the floppy disk. Do not remove the disk when this light is on.

■ To remove the floppy disk, press this button.

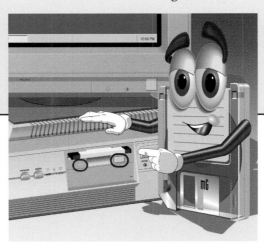

PROTECT A FLOPPY DISK

You can prevent erasing and recording information on a floppy disk by sliding the tab to the write-protected position.

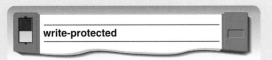

write-protected

You **cannot** erase and record information.

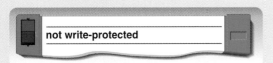

not write-protected

You **can erase** and record information.

Make sure you keep floppy disks away from magnets, which can damage the information stored on the disks. Also make sure you do not store floppy disks in extremely hot or cold locations and try not to spill liquids such as coffee or soda on the disks.

CD-ROM DRIVE

A CD-ROM drive is a device that reads information stored on Compact Discs (CDs).

Most CD-ROM drives are located inside the computer case. External CD-ROM drives that connect to the computer by a cable are also available.

CD-ROM DISC

A CD-ROM disc is the same type of disc you buy at a music store.

A single CD-ROM disc can store up to 650 MB of data. This is equal to an entire set of encyclopedias or over 400 floppy disks. The large storage capacity of CD-ROM discs provides more room for storing large images, animation and video.

CD-ROM stands for Compact Disc-Read-Only Memory. Read-only means you cannot change the information stored on a disc.

CD-ROM APPLICATIONS

Install Programs

The large storage capacity of a CD-ROM disc makes installing new programs on your computer easy. A program that requires 20 floppy disks can easily fit on a single CD-ROM disc.

Play Multimedia CD-ROM Discs

A CD-ROM disc can store multimedia presentations. Multimedia refers to the combination of text, images, sound, animation and video. Multimedia provides a powerful way of communicating information.

There are thousands of multimedia CD-ROM discs available to inform and entertain you. You can buy multimedia CD-ROM discs at most computer stores.

Play Music CDs

You can play music CDs on a CD-ROM drive while you work. Some music CDs, called Enhanced CDs, also contain multimedia you can view on your computer. For example, an Enhanced CD can include lyrics, artist interviews and music videos.

CD-ROM DRIVE

CD-ROM DRIVE SPEED

The speed of a CD-ROM drive determines how fast a disc spins. With faster speeds, information can transfer from a disc to the computer more quickly, which results in better performance.

CD-ROM drive speed is very important when viewing video and animation often found in games and encyclopedias. Slow speeds will result in jerky playback.

The speed of a CD-ROM drive is called the data transfer rate, or throughput, and is measured in Kilobytes per second (KB/s).

The chart to the right displays the most common speeds available. You should buy at least a 24X CD-ROM drive.

CD-ROM DRIVE SPEED	MAXIMUM DATA TRANSFER RATE
Eight (8X)	1,200 KB/s
Ten (10X)	1,600 KB/s
Twelve (12X)	1,800 KB/s
Sixteen (16X)	2,400 KB/s
Twenty-Four (24X)	3,600 KB/s
Thirty-Two (32X)	4,800 KB/s
Forty (40X)	6,000 KB/s
Forty-Eight (48X)	7,200 KB/s
Sixty (60X)	9,000 KB/s

WORK WITH A CD-ROM DISC

Insert a Disc

Most CD-ROM drives have a tray you use to insert a CD-ROM disc.

■ To insert or remove a disc, press this button.

■ The tray slides out. Place the disc, label side up, on the tray. To close the tray, press the button again.

A light is on when the CD-ROM drive is accessing information on the disc. Do not remove the disc or move the computer when this light is on.

Some CD-ROM drives do not have a tray. Instead, you slide the disc, label side up, into a slot in the CD-ROM drive.

Headphones

You can use headphones to listen to recorded sounds on a disc. Headphones are useful in noisy environments or when you want to listen to a disc privately.

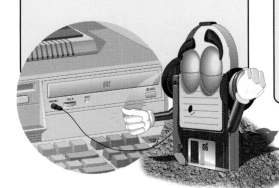

Handle a Disc

When handling a CD-ROM disc, hold the disc around the edges.

Protect a Disc

When you finish using a disc, make sure you place the disc back in its protective case. Do not stack discs on top of each other.

CD-R AND CD-RW DRIVES

CD-R and CD-RW drives are devices that allow you to store information on Compact Discs (CDs). CD-R and CD-RW drives can also play CD-ROM discs and music CDs.

CD-R DRIVE

A CD-R (Compact Disc-Recordable) drive allows you to permanently store data on a CD-R disc. CD-R discs are not erasable, so the data you record cannot be changed.

CD-RW DRIVE

A CD-RW (Compact Disc-ReWritable) drive allows you to record data on CD-RW discs. You can change the data you record on a CD-RW disc many times.

A CD-RW drive can also play and record data on CD-R discs. You can only record data on a CD-R disc once.

DRIVE SPEED

CD-R and CD-RW drives operate at several different speeds. The write speed refers to how fast a CD-R or CD-RW drive can record data onto a CD-R disc. The rewrite speed refers to how fast a CD-RW drive can record data onto a CD-RW disc. The read speed refers to how fast data transfers from a disc to the computer.

Common Drive Speeds

	CD-R	CD-RW
Write	12X	12X
Rewrite	N/A	10X
Read	24X	32X

Write Speed — Rewrite Speed — Read Speed

SOFTWARE

CD-R and CD-RW drives require special software to record data onto a disc. Most CD-R and CD-RW drives come with software specifically designed for use with the drives. You can also purchase software that provides more features, such as utilities to improve the quality of the sound you are recording.

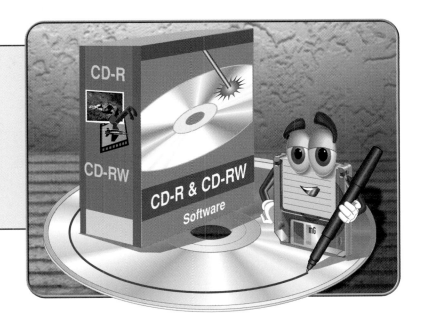

APPLICATIONS

Store and Transfer Data

CD-R and CD-RW drives allow you to store up to 650 MB of data on a single disc. This lets you easily transfer data, such as software applications or multimedia presentations, between computers. Storing data on CD-R and CD-RW discs is often referred to as "burning" a CD.

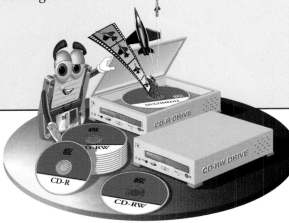

Record Music

CD-R and CD-RW drives let you record music CDs. You can find music on the Internet or you can connect a CD player or stereo system to your computer to record music. A single CD-R or CD-RW disc can usually store up to 74 minutes of music. CD-RW discs you record may not play in some CD-R and CD-ROM drives or in some CD players.

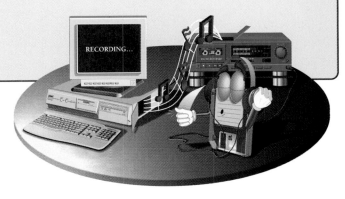

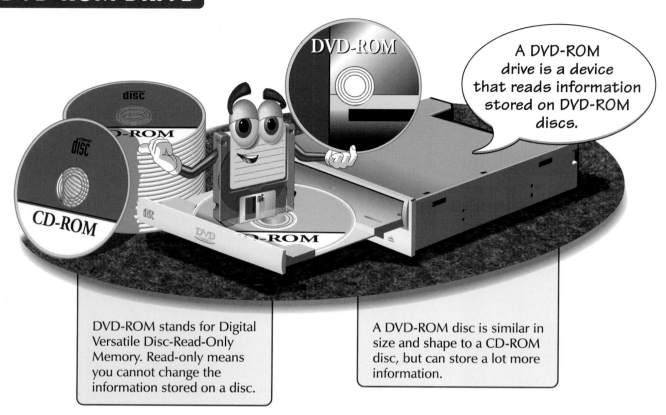

A DVD-ROM drive is a device that reads information stored on DVD-ROM discs.

DVD-ROM stands for Digital Versatile Disc-Read-Only Memory. Read-only means you cannot change the information stored on a disc.

A DVD-ROM disc is similar in size and shape to a CD-ROM disc, but can store a lot more information.

DVD-ROM APPLICATIONS

Multimedia

You can use a DVD-ROM drive to play multimedia DVD-ROM discs and CD-ROM discs, as well as music CDs. Most DVD-ROM drives can also play CD-R and CD-RW discs.

DVD-Video

DVD-ROM drives can play DVD-Video discs, which hold full-length, full-screen movies with much better quality than videocassettes. Many DVD-Video discs allow you to change the way you view the movie, such as displaying subtitles.

You may need special hardware, such as an MPEG-2 video decoder card, for the best playback of DVD-Video discs.

DVD CONSIDERATIONS

DVD Disc Storage Capacity

A single DVD disc can store at least 4.7 GB of data, which equals over seven CD-ROM discs.

Unlike a CD-ROM disc, a DVD disc can be single-sided or double-sided. Each side can store one or two layers of data.

DVD DISC	1 side/ 1 layer	1 side/ 2 layers	2 sides/ 1 layer	2 sides/ 2 layers
Storage	4.7 GB	8.5 GB	9.4 GB	17 GB

DVD-ROM Drive Speed

The speed of a DVD-ROM drive determines how quickly data can transfer from a disc to the computer. Current DVD-ROM drives commonly have a speed of 6X.

RECORDABLE DVD DRIVE

A recordable DVD drive allows you to record data on recordable DVD discs. Many recordable DVD drives are rewritable, which means that you can change the data recorded on the disc. Rewritable DVD drives are commonly called DVD-RAM drives. Most recordable DVD drives can also play CD-ROM, CD-R and CD-RW discs, as well as music CDs.

A tape drive is a device that copies files from a computer onto tape cartridges.

Tape drives are also called tape backup units.

A tape drive can be inside the computer case or connected to the computer by a cable. An external tape drive is more expensive, but can be used with more than one computer.

Tape Cartridges

A tape drive stores information on tape cartridges. These cartridges are similar to the cassettes you buy at music stores.

Store all cartridges in a cool, dry place, away from electrical equipment.

TAPE DRIVE APPLICATIONS

Back Up Data

Most people use tape drives to make backup copies of files stored on a computer. This provides extra copies in case the original files are lost or damaged due to viruses or computer failure. Most people should back up their work every day.

Archive Data

You can copy old or rarely used files from your computer to tape cartridges. You can then remove the files from your computer to provide more storage space.

Transfer Data

You can use a tape drive to transfer large amounts of information between computers. Make sure the person receiving the information uses the same type of tape drive.

BACKUP PROGRAM

A backup program helps you copy the files stored on your computer to tape cartridges.

Most tape drives come with a backup program specifically designed for use with the tape drive. Many operating systems also include a backup program.

Schedule Backups

You can set a backup program to run automatically. This lets you schedule a backup at night, when you are not using your computer.

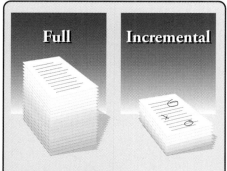

Full   **Incremental**

Types of Backups

A full backup will back up all your files. An incremental backup will back up only the files that have changed since the last backup. An incremental backup saves you time when backing up a lot of information.

Compress Data

A backup program can compress, or squeeze together, data you are backing up. This may allow you to double the amount of data you can store on a tape cartridge.

When buying a tape drive, try to find a drive that can store the entire contents of your hard drive on a single tape cartridge. This will make it easier to perform a full backup of your hard drive.

CHOOSE A TAPE DRIVE

Travan Drive

Travan drives are the most common type of tape drive. There are several levels of Travan drives and tape cartridges, including TR-1, TR-2, TR-3, TR-4 and TR-5. The higher the level, the more data the drive or tape cartridge can store. Travan drives can accept different levels of tape cartridges. A high-quality Travan drive can store up to 10 GB of data on a single Travan cartridge.

DAT Drive

A Digital Audio Tape (DAT) drive is faster than a Travan drive, but is more expensive. A high-quality DAT drive can store up to 24 GB of data on a single DAT cartridge.

TAPE CARTRIDGES TIP

Companies often advertise the amount of compressed data a tape cartridge can store. Companies assume that compression will double the amount of information a cartridge can store. This is not always the case.

TAPE CARTRIDGES

Holds **10** GB Compressed

TAPE CARTRIDGES

The amount of information that is actually compressed depends on the type of information you are storing. For example, a text file will compress significantly more than an image file.

REMOVABLE STORAGE DEVICE

A removable storage device allows you to store large amounts of data on removable disks.

A removable storage device can be inside the computer case or connected to the computer by a cable.

Removable disks are similar in size and shape to floppy disks.

TYPES OF REMOVABLE STORAGE DEVICES

Jaz Drive

Jaz drives are one of the most popular types of removable storage devices. Jaz drives are very fast and currently have the largest storage capacity of all removable storage devices. Some Jaz drives can store up to 2 GB of data on a single disk.

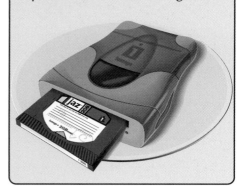

Zip Drive

Zip drives are currently a very popular type of removable storage device. A Zip drive is relatively inexpensive and can store up to 250 MB of data on a single disk.

LS-120 Drive

An LS-120 drive can store up to 120 MB of data on a single disk. Unlike many other removable storage devices, LS-120 drives also accept regular floppy disks.

REMOVABLE STORAGE DEVICE APPLICATIONS

Archive Data

You can use a removable storage device to store old or rarely used files. You can then remove the files from your computer to provide more storage space.

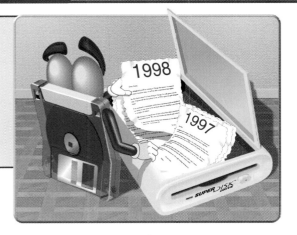

Protect Data

You can use a removable storage device to store confidential data or backup copies of data. You can then protect the data by placing the disks in a safe place on nights and weekends.

Transfer Data

You can use a removable storage device to transfer large amounts of data between computers. For example, you can take work home or transfer data to a colleague.

When using a removable storage device to transfer data, you must ensure that the person receiving the data uses the same type of device. Most removable storage devices cannot use disks from a different type of device.

CHAPTER 5

SOFTWARE

Ready to start that report? Browse through this chapter to discover how software can help you get the job done.

Game Software

Game Software

New Enhanced Sound

3-D GRAPHICS!

INTRODUCTION TO SOFTWARE

Software helps you accomplish specific tasks.

You can use software to write letters, manage your finances, draw pictures, play games and much more.

Software is also called an application or a program.

GET SOFTWARE

You can buy software at computer stores. There are also thousands of programs available on the Internet.

INSTALL SOFTWARE

Software you buy at a computer store may come on a CD-ROM disc, a DVD-ROM disc or several floppy disks. Before you can use the software, you install, or copy, the contents of the disc or disks onto your computer. Using a CD-ROM or DVD-ROM disc is a fast method of installing software.

SOFTWARE UPDATES

New Version

When a manufacturer adds new features to existing software, the updated software is given a new name or new version number. This helps people distinguish new versions of the software from older versions.

Patch

Manufacturers also may create minor software updates, called patches, to make corrections or improvements to software. A patch is also often referred to as a service pack.

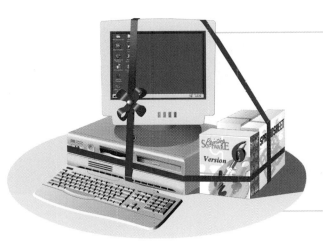

BUNDLED SOFTWARE

Bundled software is software that comes with a new computer system or device, such as a printer. Companies often include bundled software to let you start using the new equipment right away. For example, new computer systems usually come with word processing, spreadsheet and graphics programs.

GET HELP

Most software comes with a built-in help feature and printed documentation to help you learn to use the software. You can also buy computer books that contain detailed, step-by-step instructions or visit the manufacturer's Web site for more information about the software.

WORD PROCESSOR

A word processor helps you create professional-looking documents quickly and efficiently.

Commonly used word processing programs include Microsoft Word, Corel WordPerfect and Lotus Word Pro.

WORD PROCESSING BASICS

Documents

You can create many different types of documents, such as letters, reports, manuals, newsletters, brochures and Web pages.

Editing

Word processors offer many features that help you work with text in documents. You can easily add, delete or rearrange text. Most word processors also allow you to check your documents for spelling and grammar errors.

Printing

You can produce a paper copy of a document. Word processors let you see on the screen exactly what a printed document will look like.

ENHANCE A DOCUMENT

Formatting

You can easily change the appearance of text in your documents. For example, you can center text, use various fonts and create bulleted or numbered lists. You can also change the overall appearance of the pages in a document by adjusting the margin settings, adding page numbers and creating page borders.

Tables

You can create a table to neatly organize the information in a document. You can enhance the appearance of a table by adding colors and borders to the table.

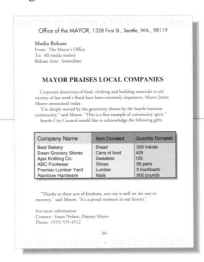

Images

Most word processors include many types of images that you can use to enhance the appearance of a document. Using images can help you draw attention to important information in a document.

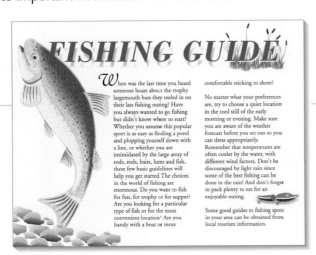

Mail Merge

Most word processors offer a merge feature that lets you quickly produce personalized letters, envelopes and mailing labels for each person on a mailing list.

SPREADSHEET

A spreadsheet program helps you manage personal and business finances.

Commonly used spreadsheet programs include Microsoft Excel, Corel Quattro Pro and Lotus 1-2-3.

SPREADSHEET APPLICATIONS

Manage Finances

You can use a spreadsheet program to perform calculations, analyze data and present information.

Manage Data in a List

A spreadsheet program lets you store a large collection of information, such as a mailing or product list. Spreadsheet programs include tools for organizing, managing, sorting and retrieving data.

If you want greater control over a list stored on your computer, use a database program. Database programs are specifically designed to manage lists of data.

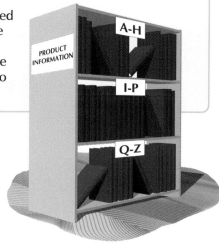

SPREADSHEET FEATURES

Editing

When working with a spreadsheet program, you can add, delete, move or copy data. Most spreadsheet programs can remember the last change you made and let you undo, or cancel, the change.

Formatting

A spreadsheet program offers many features that help you enhance the appearance of your spreadsheets. You can easily change the design and size of data. You can also add color and borders to the cells in a spreadsheet.

Formulas and Functions

Spreadsheets provide powerful formulas and functions to calculate and analyze your data. A function is a ready-to-use formula that helps you perform specialized calculations. For example, the SUM function adds a list of numbers.

Charts

A chart lets you graphically display the data in a spreadsheet. After creating a chart, you can select a new type of chart that will better suit the data.

If you later change the data used in a chart, the spreadsheet program will automatically update the chart for you.

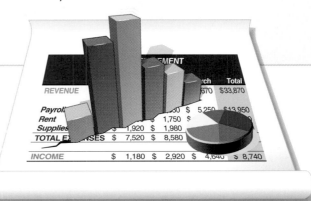

A database program helps you manage large collections of information.

Database programs are commonly used to manage mailing lists, phone directories, product listings and payroll information.

Commonly used database programs include Microsoft Access, Corel Paradox and Lotus Approach.

DATABASE BASICS

Table

A table is a collection of information about a specific topic, such as a mailing list. You can have one or more tables in a database.

Address ID	First Name	Last Name	Address	City	State/Province	Postal Code
1	Jim	Schmith	258 Linton Ave.	New York	NY	10010
2	Brenda	Petterson	50 Tree Lane	Boston	MA	02117
3	Todd	Talbot	68 Cracker Ave.	San Francisco	CA	94110
4	Chuck	Dean	47 Crosby Ave.	Las Vegas	NV	89116
5	Melanie	Robinson	26 Arnold Cres.	Jacksonville	FL	32256
6	Susan	Hughes	401 Idon Dr.	Nashville	TN	37243
7	Allen	Toppins	10 Heldon St.	Atlanta	GA	30375
8	Greg	Kilkenny	36 Buzzard St.	Boston	MA	02118
9	Jason	Marcuson	15 Bizzo Pl.	New York	NY	10020
10	Jim	Martin	890 Apple St.	San Diego	CA	92121

A table consists of fields and records.

Field

A field is a specific category of information in a table. For example, a field can contain the first names of all your clients.

Record

A record is a collection of information about one person, place or thing in a table. For example, a record can contain the name and address of one client.

DATABASE APPLICATIONS

Store Information

A database stores and manages a collection of information related to a particular subject or purpose. You can easily add, update, view and organize the information stored in a database.

Database programs provide forms you can use to quickly change the information stored in a table.

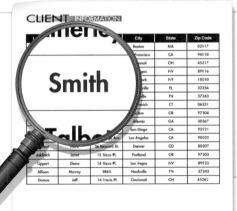

Find Information

You can instantly locate information of interest in a database. For example, you can find all clients with the last name Smith.

You can also perform more advanced searches, called queries. When you create a query, you ask a database program to find information that meets certain criteria, or conditions. For example, you can find all clients living in California who purchased more than $100 of supplies last year.

Analyze and Print Information

You can perform calculations on the information in a database to help you make quick, accurate and informed decisions.

You can neatly present the information in professionally designed reports.

An application suite is a collection of programs sold together in one package.

WORD PROCESSOR   SPREADSHEET   PRESENTATION   DATABASE

Microsoft Office is the most popular application suite. Other application suites include Corel WordPerfect Office and Lotus SmartSuite.

ADVANTAGES

Cost

Buying programs as part of an application suite costs less than buying each program individually.

Easy to Use

Programs in an application suite share a common design and work in a similar way. Once you learn one program, you can easily learn the others.

DISADVANTAGE

Since all the programs in an application suite come from the same manufacturer, you may not get the best combination of features for your needs. Make sure you evaluate all the programs in an application suite before making your purchase.

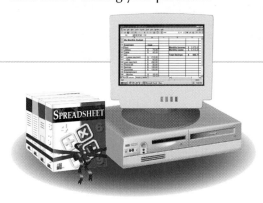

APPLICATION SUITE PROGRAMS

Application suites commonly include the following types of programs. Some application suites also offer additional programs, such as desktop publishing programs that help you design professional documents.

Word Processing Program

A word processing program lets you create documents, such as letters and reports.

Spreadsheet Program

A spreadsheet program lets you manage and analyze financial information.

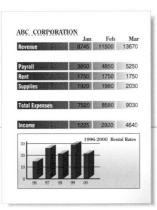

Presentation Program

A presentation program lets you design presentations.

Information Management Program

An information management program can help you manage your e-mail messages, appointments, contacts, memos and tasks.

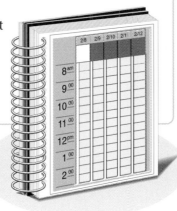

Database Program

A database program lets you manage large collections of information. A database program may only be included in higher-priced versions of an application suite.

UTILITY SOFTWARE

A utility is a program that performs a specific task on your computer.

You can buy many utility programs at computer stores. Some utility programs are also available free of charge on the Internet.

The utilities you can use depend on the operating system running on your computer.

NORTON UTILITIES

Symantec's Norton Utilities provides tools to help you maintain and optimize your computer. Norton Utilities also includes tools to help you recover lost files and protect against computer failure.

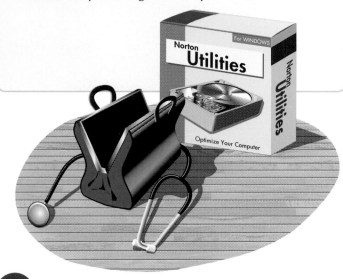

VIRUSSCAN

McAfee's VirusScan is an anti-virus program you can use to reduce the risk of a virus infecting your computer. A virus is a program that can cause problems such as affecting the performance of your computer and erasing the information on your hard drive.

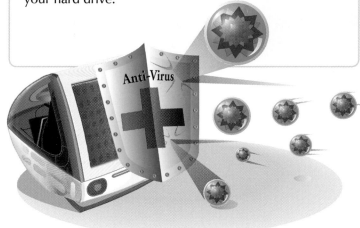

ACROBAT READER

Adobe Acrobat Reader is a program that allows you to view Portable Document Format (PDF) files. These files are often used on the World Wide Web to display books and magazines exactly as they appear in printed form.

VIAVOICE

IBM's ViaVoice is a speech recognition program that allows you to control your computer with your voice. You can speak to your computer to perform tasks such as opening files, searching the World Wide Web or dictating documents you want to create.

WINFAX PRO

With Symantec WinFax Pro, you can use your computer's fax modem to send and receive faxes. WinFax Pro allows you to convert the faxes you receive into documents you can edit using a word processor.

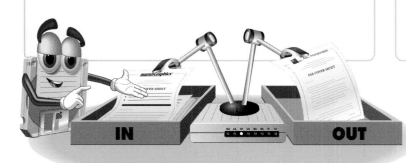

WINZIP

WinZip Computing's WinZip helps you decompress files. Many of the files on the Internet are compressed, or squeezed together, and must be decompressed before you can use them on your computer.

WinZip also compresses information so files can transfer faster between computers.

GAME SOFTWARE

Game software lets you play games on your computer.

There are many different types of games available, including action, sports, strategy, simulation, puzzle and educational games. Games are available for all ages and skill levels.

GAME CONSIDERATIONS

Purchase Games

You can buy games at computer stores. There are also many games available on the Internet. Games can be very expensive, but game manufacturers often offer a trial version, or demo version, of their games for free on the World Wide Web. This allows you to try a game before you buy it.

Internet and Network Games

Many games are designed to let multiple people compete against each other on the Internet or on a network.

There are many online gaming services available that allow you to easily connect to other people on the Internet to play a game. When you play a game with other people on the Internet, each person usually has to have their own copy of the game.

You may need special hardware to use game software on your computer.

GAME HARDWARE

Game Controller

A game controller is a device, such as a joystick or gamepad, which allows you to interact with a game. Popular game controllers include Microsoft SideWinder and Gravis GamePad.

Some games require a specific type of game controller. Before buying a game, check to see what type of controller the game requires.

3D Graphics Accelerator Card

Many games are designed with 3D graphics and run best on a computer with a 3D graphics card.

A 3D graphics card is a circuit board that translates complex instructions from the computer into a form the monitor can understand. Popular 3D graphics cards include Matrox Millennium, ATI Radeon and 3dfx Voodoo.

Some games require a specific type of 3D graphics card. Before buying a game, check to see what type of card the game requires.

CHAPTER 6

OPERATING SYSTEMS

**What is an operating system and which
one is best for you? This chapter provides
the information you are looking for.**

An operating system is the software that controls the overall activity of a computer.

An operating system ensures that all parts of a computer system work together smoothly and efficiently.

OPERATING SYSTEM FUNCTIONS

Control Hardware

An operating system controls the different parts of a computer system and enables all the parts to work together.

Run Software

An operating system runs software, such as Microsoft Word and Corel Quattro Pro.

Manage Information

An operating system provides ways to manage and organize information stored on a computer. You can use an operating system to sort, copy, move, delete or view files.

TYPES OF OPERATING SYSTEMS

MS-DOS

MS-DOS stands for Microsoft Disk Operating System. MS-DOS displays lines of text on the screen. You perform tasks by typing text commands.

Windows

Windows is a Graphical User Interface (GUI, pronounced "gooey"). A GUI allows you to use pictures instead of text commands to perform tasks. This makes Windows easier to use than MS-DOS.

UNIX

UNIX is a powerful operating system used by many computers on the Internet. There are many different versions of the UNIX operating system available.

Mac OS

Mac OS is a Graphical User Interface (GUI) for Macintosh computers.

PLATFORM

A platform refers to the type of operating system used by a computer, such as Windows or UNIX. Programs used on one platform will not usually work on another platform. For example, you cannot use Word for Windows on a computer running UNIX.

MS-DOS

MS-DOS is an operating system that performs tasks using text commands you enter.

MS-DOS stands for Microsoft Disk Operating System.

ENTER A COMMAND

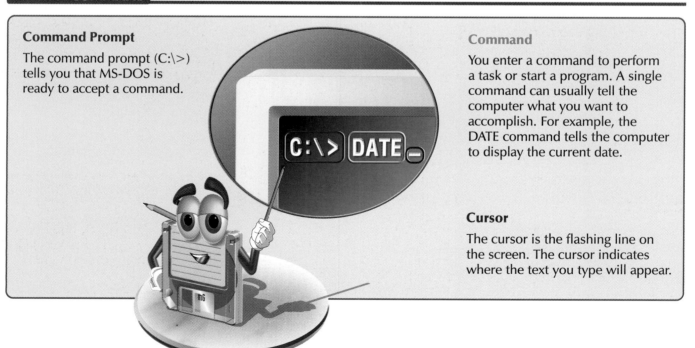

Command Prompt

The command prompt (C:\>) tells you that MS-DOS is ready to accept a command.

Command

You enter a command to perform a task or start a program. A single command can usually tell the computer what you want to accomplish. For example, the DATE command tells the computer to display the current date.

Cursor

The cursor is the flashing line on the screen. The cursor indicates where the text you type will appear.

FILE ORGANIZATION

Like folders in a filing cabinet, MS-DOS uses directories to organize the data stored on a computer.

The root directory (C:\) is the main directory. All other directories are located within this directory.

A path describes the location of a file.

■ The path for this file is C:\letters\personal\john.let

FILE NAME

When you store a file on a computer, you must give the file a name. An MS-DOS file name cannot contain any spaces. A file name consists of a name and an extension, separated by a period.

The **name** describes the contents of a file and can have up to eight characters.

The **extension** identifies the type of file and consists of three characters.

UTILITIES

Some versions of MS-DOS include special programs, called utilities, to protect files and optimize a computer.

For example, the ScanDisk program finds and repairs disk errors.

Windows 3.1 works with MS-DOS to control the overall activity of a computer. Windows 3.1 is not a true operating system since it needs MS-DOS to operate.

Windows 3.1 displays pictures on the screen to help you perform tasks.

Program Manager

The Program Manager is the control center where you start programs.

Program Icon

A program icon lets you start a program, such as a word processor. An icon is a small picture that represents an item, such as a program.

Window

A window is a rectangle that displays information on the screen. Each window has a title bar that displays the name of the window (example: Accessories).

Group Icon

A group icon contains program icons. For example, the Games group icon contains several games.

File Manager

The File Manager lets you view and organize all the files stored on your computer. Windows 3.1 uses directories to organize information, just as you would use folders to organize papers in a filing cabinet.

Desktop

The desktop is the background area of the screen.

> Windows 95 is the successor to Windows 3.1. This operating system is more graphical and easier to use than Windows 3.1.

Windows 95 is a true operating system because it does not need MS-DOS to operate.

My Computer

My Computer lets you browse through all the folders and documents stored on your computer.

Recycle Bin

The Recycle Bin stores documents you delete and allows you to recover them later.

Network Neighborhood

Network Neighborhood lets you view the folders and files available on your network.

Start Button

The Start button lets you quickly access programs and documents.

Taskbar

The taskbar contains the Start button and displays the name of each open window on the screen.

Windows Explorer

Windows Explorer shows you the location of each folder and document on your computer. You can use Windows Explorer to move, open, print or delete documents.

Shortcut

A shortcut provides a quick way to open a document or program you use regularly.

Windows 98 is the successor to Windows 95. This operating system is very similar to Windows 95 but includes many new and improved features.

There are currently two versions of Windows 98. Windows 98 Second Edition includes many enhancements and updates to the original version of Windows 98.

You can check your Windows 98 CD-ROM disc to determine whether you have Windows 98 Second Edition installed on your computer.

My Documents

My Documents provides a convenient place to store your documents.

Internet Explorer

Internet Explorer lets you browse through information on the World Wide Web.

Quick Launch Toolbar

The Quick Launch Toolbar lets you quickly access commonly used features, including Internet Explorer and Outlook Express.

WINDOWS 98 FEATURES

Computer Maintenance

Windows 98 is more reliable than Windows 95 and includes many tools you can use to find and fix problems with your computer. For example, you can check your hard drive for errors, remove unnecessary files and defragment your hard drive to improve its performance.

FAT32

FAT32 is a file system that better manages data on large hard drives to reduce wasted space. Windows 98 can convert your hard drive to FAT32 without disrupting your current programs and documents.

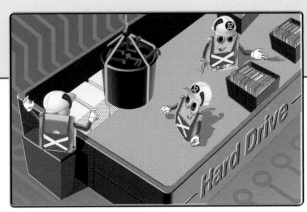

Multiple Monitor Capability

Windows 98 has the ability to display the Windows desktop on multiple monitors. This makes working with several open documents or programs easier.

Internet

Windows 98 includes several programs that allow you to view and exchange information on the Internet, including Internet Explorer, Outlook Express and FrontPage Express. Outlook Express lets you exchange electronic mail with people around the world. FrontPage Express allows you to create your own Web pages.

WINDOWS ME

> Windows Me is the successor to Windows 98. Windows Me stands for Windows Millennium Edition.

If you have used Windows 98, you will already be familiar with the way Windows Me looks and works.

WINDOWS ME FEATURES

Record Videos

Windows Me allows you to record, edit and save videos on your computer using Windows Movie Maker. Once you have finished working with a video, you can e-mail the video to your friends and colleagues or place the video on a Web page.

Manage Multimedia Files

Windows Me contains an enhanced version of Windows Media Player that helps you manage your multimedia files. You can use Windows Media Player to play a variety of multimedia files and listen to radio stations over the Internet.

Restore Your Computer

If you are experiencing problems with your computer, you can use the System Restore feature to return your computer to a time before the problems occurred. For example, if you have accidentally deleted program files, you can restore your computer to a time before you deleted the files.

Set Up a Home Network

If you have more than one computer at home, you can use the Home Networking Wizard to help you set up a network so you can exchange information between the computers. A home network is also useful for sharing equipment and playing multiplayer games.

Update Windows

The Windows Update feature allows you to automatically update your computer with the latest Windows features available on the Internet. When you are connected to the Internet, Windows will automatically check for updates, determine which updates apply to your computer and notify you when the updates are available.

WINDOWS NT

Windows NT is a powerful version of the Windows operating system that provides advanced networking and security features.

Windows NT is available in two main versions.

Windows NT Workstation

Windows NT Workstation is a version of the Windows NT operating system that is used on client/server and some peer-to-peer networks.

Many powerful applications are designed specifically to run on Windows NT Workstation. Many programs designed for the Windows 95 and Windows 98 operating systems will also perform better on Windows NT Workstation.

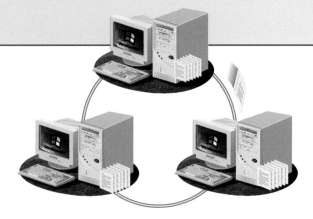

Windows NT Server

Windows NT Server is a version of the Windows NT operating system that is used on client/server networks. Windows NT Server is designed to support the heavy processing demands of a network server.

The client computers on a network running Windows NT Server can use a variety of operating systems, such as Linux, Windows 98 and Mac OS 9.

Windows 2000 is the successor to Windows NT. This operating system offers improved networking and security features.

There are several versions of Windows 2000 available.

Windows 2000 Professional

Windows 2000 Professional is commonly used on client/server networks but can also be used on peer-to-peer networks. This operating system offers increased stability and provides tools that can help you maintain your computer. Windows 2000 Professional is intended for business use.

Windows 2000 Server and Windows 2000 Advanced Server

Windows 2000 Server and Windows 2000 Advanced Server are found on large client/server networks. These operating systems are both designed to support heavy network processing demands. Windows 2000 Advanced Server can support a larger network than Windows 2000 Server, which makes the Advanced Server version suitable for large businesses and Internet service providers.

UNIX

UNIX is an older, powerful operating system that can be used to run a single computer or an entire network.

UNIX is the oldest computer operating system still in widespread use today.

VERSIONS

Many companies have owned UNIX since its development in the late 1960s. Today, there are several versions of the UNIX operating system available.

Popular UNIX operating systems for personal computers include UnixWare by SCO, Solaris by Sun Microsystems and Linux, which is available for free on the World Wide Web. Other versions of UNIX that are more popular as network operating systems include HP-UX by Hewlett-Packard and AIX by IBM.

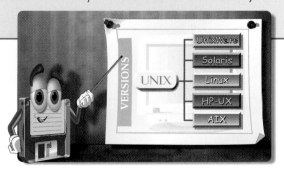

INTERNET

Many of the first computers used to establish the Internet ran the UNIX operating system. Even today, UNIX is the most widely used operating system for servers on the Internet.

UNIX FEATURES

Power

The UNIX operating system is very powerful. UNIX is harder to install and set up than most other operating systems, but provides greater control over a computer's resources and power.

A computer's performance may be significantly improved when running UNIX.

Multitasking

UNIX was originally developed as the operating system for a single large computer, called a mainframe computer. Since multiple users can access a mainframe computer at the same time, UNIX was developed to run many programs and perform numerous tasks at once, called multitasking.

UNIX's multitasking capabilities make it an efficient operating system for networks.

Security

UNIX has many built-in security features to protect information from being accidentally deleted or accessed by unauthorized users.

UNIX's strong security features are one of the reasons UNIX is such a popular operating system on the Internet.

Linux is a UNIX-based operating system that is available for free on the World Wide Web.

Many companies, such as Red Hat, Corel and Mandrake, create easy-to-use versions of Linux that you can purchase.

Red Hat Linux is a popular version of Linux that comes with the GNOME desktop environment. GNOME displays pictures on the screen to help you perform tasks.

Home directory

The Home directory allows you to browse through the folder that stores your personal files.

Help Web Pages

The Help Web pages let you quickly display Web pages that offer help on using Linux.

GNOME Panel

The GNOME Panel contains the Main Menu button and Application Launchers and displays the name of each open window on the screen.

Main Menu Button

The Main Menu button gives you quick access to programs.

Application Launchers

Application Launchers allow you to quickly access commonly used programs, such as the help system and Netscape Communicator.

LINUX FEATURES

Software

Red Hat Linux includes a wide variety of software, such as a drawing program, spreadsheet program, calendar program and a simple text editor. You will also find an on-screen calculator, an address book and many games that you can play.

Accounts

When you install Linux, the root account and one or more user accounts are created. You can work in Linux using either the root account or a personal account. The root account is useful for performing administrative and maintenance tasks. When performing daily tasks, you should work in a user account. You can set up a different user account for each person who uses your computer.

Command Line

You can work in Linux using a Graphical User Interface (GUI) such as GNOME or using the command line. The command line displays text without any graphics. Working in the command line allows you to perform many tasks more quickly than in a GUI, though you must know the proper commands.

MAC OS 9

> Mac OS 9 is a popular version of the Macintosh operating system.

This operating system offers many advanced multimedia and Internet features.

MAC OS 9 FEATURES

Multimedia

Mac OS 9 offers advanced sound, video and graphics capabilities. For example, the QuickTime player allows you to manage and play multimedia files, such as songs and movie clips. Mac OS 9 also offers a speech recognition program that allows your computer to recognize voice commands.

Internet

Mac OS 9 offers several features that help you find and exchange information on the Internet. For example, the Sherlock 2 feature allows you to efficiently search for information in categories such as News, Reference, People and Shopping.

Mac OS X (ten) is the latest version of the Macintosh operating system.

MAC OS X FEATURES

Graphical User Interface

Mac OS X offers a new Graphical User Interface (GUI) that is designed to make the operating system easier to use than previous versions. The new GUI features photo-quality icons and an area at the bottom of the screen, called the Dock, where you can store items you frequently access.

Graphics

Mac OS X combines several advanced graphics technologies, including Portable Document Format (PDF), QuickTime and OpenGL, to provide enhanced graphics capabilities. This improves the display of graphics in programs such as desktop publishing programs and games.

Operating System Core

Mac OS X offers an improved operating system core, or kernel. This improved kernel helps ensure that your computer hardware and software work together efficiently and provides more stability than previous versions of the Macintosh operating system.

CHAPTER 7

PORTABLE COMPUTERS

Wondering what to look for in a portable computer? This chapter will provide all the information you need.

INTRODUCTION TO NOTEBOOK COMPUTERS

A notebook is a small, lightweight computer that you can easily transport.

You can buy a notebook computer with the same capabilities as a full-sized computer, although notebook computers are more expensive.

PROGRAM 2.1
CD-ROM

A notebook computer is also called a laptop.

A notebook computer has a built-in keyboard, pointing device and screen. This eliminates the need for cables to connect these devices to the notebook.

ADVANTAGES OF NOTEBOOKS

Travel

A notebook computer lets you work when traveling or outdoors. You can also use a notebook computer to bring work home instead of staying late at the office.

Presentations

You can bring a notebook computer to meetings to present information.

BATTERY

A battery or an electrical outlet can supply the power for a notebook computer.

A battery lets you use a notebook when no electrical outlets are available.

TYPES OF BATTERIES

There are two main types of batteries–nickel metal hydride (NiMH) and lithium-ion. Lithium-ion is a more expensive battery, but is lighter and lasts longer than NiMH. Some notebook computers now use Smart batteries. Smart batteries help notebooks better manage power consumption.

MONITOR A BATTERY

Most notebooks display the amount of battery power remaining, either on the screen or on a panel built into the computer.

RECHARGE A BATTERY

The power supplied by most batteries lasts for only a few hours. You must recharge a battery before you can use it again. If you are unable to recharge a battery when traveling, bring an extra battery so you can work for a longer period of time.

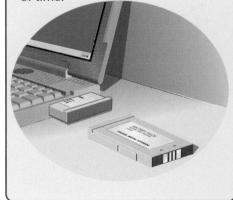

The screen on a notebook computer uses Liquid Crystal Display (LCD). This is the same type of display found in most digital wristwatches.

An LCD screen uses very little power, which extends the length of time you can use a battery before needing to recharge. An LCD screen also weighs much less than a full-size monitor, which makes a notebook easier to carry.

BACKLIGHT

Notebooks have an internal light source that illuminates the back of the screen. This makes the screen easier to view in poorly lit areas but shortens the length of time you can use a battery before needing to recharge.

USE A FULL-SIZE MONITOR

Most notebooks can use both the notebook screen and a full-size monitor at the same time. This feature is very useful when delivering presentations.

SCREEN SIZE

The size of the screen is measured diagonally. Screen sizes range from about 12 to 15 inches.

TYPES OF SCREENS

Passive Matrix

This type of screen is less expensive than an active matrix screen, but is not as bright or rich in color. The lower cost makes a passive matrix screen ideal for routine office tasks.

A dual-scan screen is an enhanced version of a passive matrix screen that offers improved clarity.

Passive matrix screens can be difficult to read when viewed from an angle. This is ideal when you want to keep work private from people sitting next to you on a train or plane, but makes delivering a presentation to several people difficult.

Active Matrix

This type of screen is more expensive, but displays brighter, richer colors than a passive matrix screen.

An active matrix screen is also called a Thin-Film Transistor (TFT) screen.

You can view an active matrix screen from wide angles, which makes it more suitable for delivering presentations to several people.

INPUT AND OUTPUT DEVICES

There are several devices that let you move the pointer around the screen of a notebook computer.

A mouse is impractical when traveling, since you need a relatively large, flat surface to move the mouse.

Pointing Stick

A pointing stick is a small device that resembles an eraser. You push a pointing stick in different directions to move the pointer on the screen.

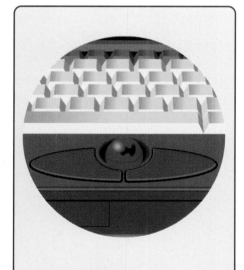

Trackball

A trackball is an upside-down mouse that remains stationary. You roll the ball with your fingers or palm to move the pointer on the screen.

Touchpad

A touchpad is a surface that is sensitive to pressure and motion. When you move your fingertip across the pad, the pointer on the screen moves in the same direction.

KEYBOARD

The keys on a notebook keyboard may be small and close together to save space. Before buying a notebook, type several paragraphs of text to make sure the keyboard is suitable for you.

Some notebook computers have a keyboard that expands to a full-size keyboard.

MODEM

You can buy a notebook with a built-in modem or add modem capabilities later.

A modem allows you to connect to the Internet to exchange information and messages.

When traveling, a modem also lets you connect to the network at work.

SOUND CARD AND SPEAKERS

You can buy a notebook with a built-in sound card and speakers to play and record sound. This is very useful when you want to use the notebook to deliver presentations.

STORAGE DEVICES

HARD DRIVE

The hard drive is the primary device a notebook uses to store information. Buy the largest hard drive you can afford. New programs and data will quickly fill a hard drive.

CD-ROM OR DVD-ROM DRIVE

A notebook computer can include a CD-ROM drive or a DVD-ROM drive to read information stored on Compact Discs (CDs) or Digital Versatile Discs (DVDs).

Some notebooks let you remove the CD-ROM or DVD-ROM drive and replace it with another component. This new component could be an extra battery to increase the amount of time you can use the notebook, a second hard drive for additional storage space or a floppy drive.

FLOPPY DRIVE

Many notebooks come with a floppy drive to store and retrieve information on floppy disks.

If you will not use a floppy drive very often, you can buy a notebook without a floppy drive to reduce the notebook's weight. You can then connect the notebook to an external floppy drive when necessary.

PROCESSING

The Central Processing Unit (CPU) is the main chip in a computer. The CPU processes instructions, performs calculations and manages the flow of information through a computer system.

CPU

Special CPUs, called mobile CPUs, are developed for notebook computers. Mobile CPUs are smaller and consume less power than traditional CPUs.

This chart shows common CPUs available for notebook computers. The CPU you decide to buy will depend on your budget and how you plan to use the computer.

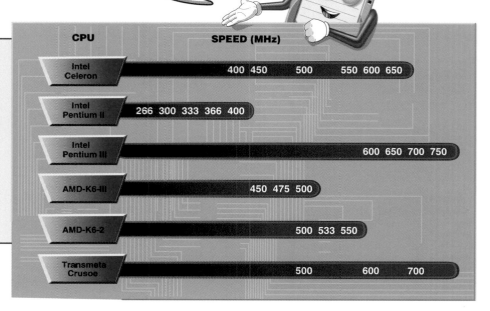

CPU	SPEED (MHz)
Intel Celeron	400 450 500 550 600 650
Intel Pentium II	266 300 333 366 400
Intel Pentium III	600 650 700 750
AMD-K6-III	450 475 500
AMD-K6-2	500 533 550
Transmeta Crusoe	500 600 700

MEMORY

Electronic memory, or RAM, temporarily stores data inside a computer. Memory works like a blackboard that is constantly overwritten with new data. A notebook computer running Windows Me should have at least 32 MB of memory to ensure that programs run smoothly.

PC CARD

A PC Card adds a new capability, such as memory, to a notebook computer.

Some PC Cards provide multiple features. For example, a single PC Card can provide networking and modem capabilities.

A PC Card used to be called a PCMCIA Card. PCMCIA stands for Personal Computer Memory Card International Association.

TYPES OF PC CARDS

A PC Card is a lightweight device about the size of a credit card. There are three types of PC Cards—Type I, Type II and Type III. Type I is the thinnest card, while Type III is the thickest. Each type of card can vary in the features it offers.

PC SLOT

You insert a PC Card into a slot on a notebook computer. Most notebook computers have a PC slot that can accept both a Type I and Type II PC Card or one Type III PC Card.

NETWORK INTERFACE CARD

A network interface card connects a notebook to a network and controls the flow of information between the network and the notebook. When connected to a network, you can access all the equipment and information available on the network.

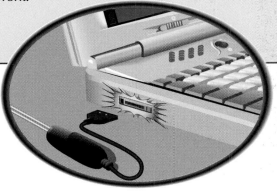

INFRARED PORT

Some notebook computers have an infrared port to share information without using cables. Infrared ports are commonly used for connecting a notebook computer to a printer.

PORT REPLICATOR

A port replicator lets you connect many devices, such as a printer, modem and mouse, to a notebook at once. After you connect a port replicator to a notebook, you can use all the devices attached to the port replicator without having to attach each device to the notebook individually.

DOCKING STATION

A docking station lets you connect many devices to a notebook at once. A docking station can also provide additional features, such as networking capabilities and a full-size monitor and keyboard.

INTRODUCTION TO HANDHELD COMPUTERS

A handheld computer is a portable computer small enough to carry in your hand.

A handheld computer is also called a Personal Digital Assistant (PDA) or pocket computer.

Popular handheld computers include Palm Inc's Palm computers and Handspring's Visor.

INPUT DEVICES

Stylus

Instead of a mouse, handheld computers use an electronic pen, called a stylus, to select objects on the screen.

Keyboard

You can purchase a collapsible keyboard for some types of handheld computers. This lets you type information into the handheld computer.

Wireless Modem

You can add wireless modem capabilities to some types of handheld computers. This allows you to exchange electronic mail and access information from your network at work while traveling.

OPERATING SYSTEMS

Most handheld computers use either the Palm OS® or Windows CE operating system to control the overall activity of the computer. Palm OS and Windows CE are Graphical User Interfaces (GUI, pronounced "gooey"). A GUI allows you to use pictures instead of text commands to perform tasks.

HANDHELD COMPUTER APPLICATIONS

Electronic Organizers

Handheld computers are capable of storing thousands of addresses, appointments and memos. Most handheld computers also come with scheduling software, such as a calendar program.

Exchange Information

You can connect a handheld computer to a desktop computer to exchange data between the two computers. Some handheld computers have infrared technology, which allows them to exchange information with other handheld computers without having to be connected.

OTHER HANDHELD COMPUTERS

Some cell phones and pagers now offer computing capabilities. For example, these devices may offer scheduling software and allow you to access the Internet and exchange electronic mail.

RIM's BlackBerry is a popular handheld device that allows you to send and receive electronic mail.

CHAPTER 8

MACINTOSH COMPUTERS

Wondering what a Mac is? This chapter will introduce you to Macintosh computers.

INTRODUCTION TO MACINTOSH COMPUTERS

Macintosh computers, or Macs, were introduced by Apple Computer in 1984.

Macintosh computers were the first home computers with a mouse, on-screen windows, menus and icons.

MACINTOSH ADVANTAGES

Easy to Use

The graphical interface of a Macintosh makes this type of computer very easy to use.

Desktop Publishing

The fast display of images on screen and true What You See Is What You Get (WYSIWYG) display have helped to establish Macintosh computers as the standard in the desktop publishing industry. Desktop publishing lets you create professional documents by integrating text and graphics on a page.

TYPES OF MACINTOSH COMPUTERS

There are many types of Macintosh computers available, including Power Macs, the iMac and notebook computers.

POWER MAC

The latest Power Mac, called the G4, is a tower computer that comes with powerful processing capabilities. You can easily expand the capabilities of the Power Mac G4 as your needs increase.

Apple also manufactures the Power Mac Cube, which is less than a quarter of the size of most tower computers.

iMAC

The iMac is an all-in-one computer. An all-in-one computer contains many devices, such as a monitor, CD-ROM drive and speakers, in a single unit. The iMac is easy for beginners to set up and use.

NOTEBOOKS

The PowerBook and iBook are notebook computers. Like other notebook computers, the PowerBook and iBook are lightweight and come with a built-in keyboard and screen. You can buy a PowerBook with the same capabilities as a full-sized computer.

OPERATING SYSTEM

An operating system is the software that controls the overall activity of a computer.

Like the Windows operating systems, Macintosh operating systems use a Graphical User Interface (GUI, pronounced "gooey"). A GUI allows you to use pictures instead of text commands to perform tasks.

VERSIONS

Mac OS 9

Many Macintosh computers currently use the Mac OS 9 operating system, which offers advanced Internet features. The Mac OS 9 operating system improves on previous versions of the Macintosh operating system, such as Mac OS 8.

Mac OS X

The latest version of the Macintosh operating system is Mac OS X. This version offers many new features, including a new graphical user interface. The new technologies offered by Mac OS X make it a worthwhile upgrade from Mac OS 9.

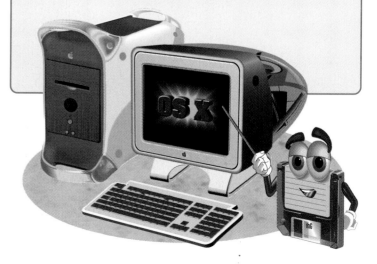

PORT

A port is a connector at the back of a computer where you plug in an external device.

FireWire

Most new Macintosh computers come with one or two FireWire ports. A FireWire port allows you to attach up to 63 devices to your computer using a single port. FireWire connections are faster than other types of connections, which makes them ideal for connecting multimedia and high-speed devices such as video cameras, digital cameras and external hard drives.

Network Port

A network port connects the computer to a network.

USB Port

Most Macintosh computers come with one or two Universal Serial Bus (USB) ports. A USB port allows you to connect up to 127 devices using a single port. For example, you can use a USB port to connect a printer, modem and joystick to your computer.

Speaker Port

A speaker port connects speakers.

Microphone Port

A microphone port connects a microphone.

Monitor Port

A monitor port connects a monitor.

INPUT AND OUTPUT DEVICES

MOUSE

A mouse is a handheld pointing device that lets you select and move items on your screen. Unlike a PC mouse, which has two buttons, a Macintosh mouse has only one button.

KEYBOARD

The keys on a keyboard let you enter information and instructions into a computer. The Macintosh keyboard has a **Command**, or **Apple**, key ( ) that you can use to quickly perform specific tasks. For example, in a word processing document, you can quickly make text bold by pressing the and **B** keys.

MONITOR

A monitor displays text and images generated by a computer. Some monitors are designed to work only with Macintosh computers. For more flexibility, you can buy a monitor that will work with both Macs and PCs.

VIDEO CAPABILITIES

All Macintosh computers come with built-in video capabilities that translate instructions from the computer into a form the monitor can understand.

SOUND CAPABILITIES

All Macintosh computers come with built-in sound capabilities. This allows Macintosh computers to play and record sound.

MODEM

A modem lets computers exchange information through telephone lines. Most Macintosh modems are built-in modems.

PRINTER

A printer produces a paper copy of the information displayed on the screen. When buying a printer for a Macintosh computer, make sure the printer is Macintosh-compatible. A printer designed for a PC may not work with a Mac.

IMAGING DEVICE

You can purchase an imaging device for your Macintosh computer, such as a scanner, video camera or digital camera. A scanner is a device that reads images and text into a computer. A video camera or digital camera lets you store videos or pictures on your computer.

Scanner

Video Camera

Digital Camera

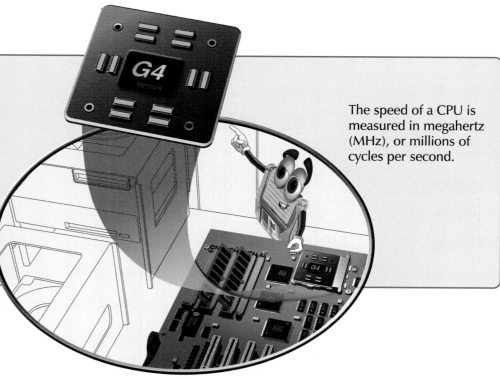

CPU

The Central Processing Unit (CPU), also called a microprocessor, is the main chip in a computer. A CPU processes instructions, performs calculations and manages the flow of information through a computer system.

All new Macintosh computers use PowerPC microprocessors, also called Reduced Instruction Set Computer (RISC) chips.

The speed of a CPU is measured in megahertz (MHz), or millions of cycles per second.

Types of CPUs

G3

The PowerPC G3 microprocessor is currently used in many Macintosh computers, including the PowerBook and iBook notebook computers. This CPU can have speeds ranging from 300 to 500 MHz.

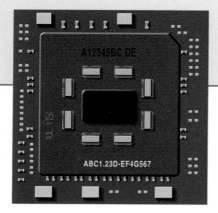

G4

High-performance Apple computers, such as Power Macs, use the PowerPC G4 microprocessor. Some Power Macs contain two G4 microprocessors, offering increased processing speed and power.

The G4 microprocessor allows computers to efficiently perform complex tasks such as creating multimedia files and performing large calculations. The G4 microprocessor was one of the first CPUs to perform over a billion calculations in a second.

BUS

The bus is the electronic pathway in a computer that carries information between devices.

The efficiency of a bus depends on the bus width and the bus speed. Bus speed is measured in megahertz (MHz), or millions of cycles per second.

PCI Bus

Macintosh computers use the Peripheral Component Interconnect (PCI) bus. The PCI bus can have a width of 32 or 64 bits and a speed of up to 66 MHz.

MEMORY

Memory, also called Random Access Memory (RAM), temporarily stores data inside a computer.

The amount of memory determines the number of programs a computer can run at once and how fast programs will operate.

Capacity

Memory is measured in bytes. You should buy a Macintosh with at least 64 MB of memory, but 128 MB of memory is recommended. You can often improve the performance of a computer by adding more memory.

CHAPTER 9

NETWORKS

How can multiple computers share information more efficiently? Learn about networks in this chapter.

INTRODUCTION TO NETWORKS

> A network is a group of connected computers that allows people to share information and equipment.

LOCAL AREA NETWORK

A Local Area Network (LAN) is a network that connects computers within a small geographic area, such as a building.

Home Network

A home network is a small local area network that connects computers in a home. Home networks are often used to play multi-player games. There are home networking kits available that contain all the necessary hardware and software for creating a home network.

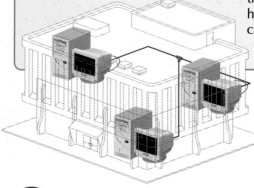

WIDE AREA NETWORK

A Wide Area Network (WAN) is a network that connects computers across a large geographic area, such as a city or country. A WAN can transmit information by telephone line, microwave or satellite.

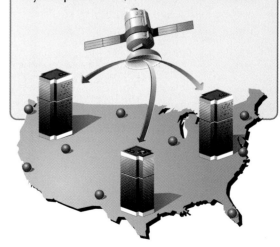

NETWORK ADVANTAGES

Work Away From Office

When traveling or at home, you can connect to the network at work to exchange messages and files.

Eliminate Sneakernet

Sneakernet refers to physically carrying information from one computer to another to exchange information. A computer network eliminates the need for sneakernet.

Share Information

Networks let you easily share data and programs. You can exchange documents, electronic mail, video, sound and images.

Share Equipment

Computers connected to a network can share equipment, such as a printer or modem.

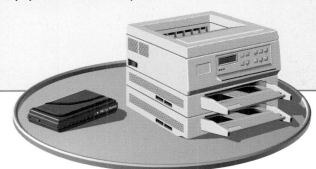

NETWORK ADMINISTRATOR

A network administrator manages the network and makes sure the network runs smoothly. A network administrator may also be called a network manager, information systems manager or system administrator.

Network Administrator

NETWORK APPLICATIONS

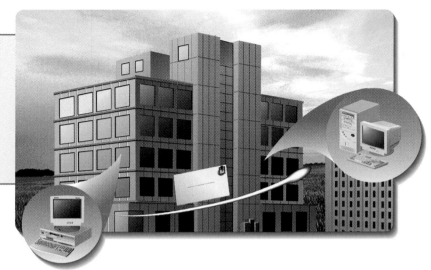

ELECTRONIC MAIL

You can exchange electronic mail (e-mail) messages with other people on a network. Electronic mail saves paper and provides a fast, convenient way to exchange ideas and request information.

GROUPWARE

Groupware is software that helps people on a network coordinate and manage projects. Groupware packages usually let you exchange electronic mail, schedule meetings, participate in online discussions and share corporate information. Popular groupware packages include Lotus Domino and Novell GroupWise.

VIDEOCONFERENCING

Videoconferencing allows you to have face-to-face conversations with other people on a network, whether they are in the same building or on the other side of the country.

A computer must have a sound card, speakers and a microphone to transmit and receive sound. The computer must also have a video camera to transmit video images.

Computers

A network links computers together, allowing the people using the computers to work more efficiently. A network can connect different types of computers, such as IBM-compatible and Macintosh computers.

Hub

A hub is a device that provides a central location where all the cables on a network come together.

Network Interface Card

A network interface card is an expansion card that physically connects each computer to a network. This card controls the flow of information between the network and the computer.

Cables

Cables are the wires that connect computers and equipment on a network. There are four main types of cables—coaxial, Unshielded Twisted Pair (UTP), Shielded Twisted Pair (STP) and fiber-optic.

Fiber-optic cable is the most expensive type of cable, but it can carry information faster and over longer distances than other cables.

The people on a peer-to-peer network store their files on their own computers. Anyone on the network can access shared files stored on another computer.

PEER-TO-PEER NETWORK

A peer-to-peer network provides a simple and inexpensive way to connect fewer than ten computers.

Manage Files

The files on a peer-to-peer network are stored in many different locations. This makes the files difficult to manage, back up and protect. However, if one computer malfunctions, the rest of the network will not be affected.

Popular Operating Systems

Popular operating systems that provide peer-to-peer networking capabilities include LANtastic, Windows 98 and Windows Me.

The people on a client/server network store their files on a central computer. Everyone connected to the network can access files stored on the central computer.

CLIENT/SERVER NETWORK

A client/server network provides a highly efficient way to connect ten or more computers, or computers that exchange large amounts of information.

Server

The server is the central computer that stores the files of every person on the network.

Manage Files

All the files on a client/server network are stored on the server. This makes the files easy to manage, back up and protect. However, if the server malfunctions, the entire network will be affected.

Client

A client is a computer that can access information stored on the server.

Popular Operating Systems

Popular operating systems that provide client/server networking capabilities include NetWare and Windows 2000.

ETHERNET

Ethernet is the most popular and least expensive way information can travel through a network. Ethernet is the easiest type of network to set up.

How Ethernet Works

Ethernet works the same way people talk during a polite conversation. Each computer waits for a pause before sending information through a network.

Speed

Ethernet can transfer information through a network at a speed of 10 megabits per second (Mbps). Fast Ethernet can transfer information through a network at a speed of 100 Mbps. Gigabit Ethernet is a new type of Ethernet that can transfer information through a network at a speed of 1000 Mbps.

When two computers try to send information at the same time, a collision occurs. After a moment, the computers resend the information.

Token-ring is a type of network often found in large organizations, such as banks and insurance companies.

TOKEN-RING

How Token-ring Works

Token-ring works by passing a single token from computer to computer. The token collects and delivers information as it travels around the network.

Speed

A token-ring network can send information through a network at speeds of 4 or 16 Mbps.

Asynchronous Transfer Mode (ATM) is a faster, more powerful way to exchange information on busy networks.

ATM

Companies often use ATM to transfer information between two separate networks.

How ATM Works

ATM works by sending information in equal-sized pieces, called cells.

Speed

ATM can send information at speeds of 25, 155, 622 or 2488 Mbps.

FIREWALL

A firewall is special software or hardware designed to protect a private computer network from unauthorized access and viruses. Corporations, banks and research facilities use firewalls to keep information private and secure.

USER NAME AND PASSWORD

You usually have to enter a user name and password when you want to access information on a network. This ensures that only authorized people can use the information stored on the network.

Choose a Password

When choosing a password, do not use words that people can easily associate with you, such as your name or favorite sport. The most effective password connects two words or number sequences with a special character (example: easy@123). To increase security, memorize your password and do not write it down.

An intranet is a small version of the Internet within a company or organization.

Distribute Information

An intranet is a very efficient and inexpensive way to make internal company documents available to employees. Companies use intranets to distribute information such as phone directories, product listings and job openings.

Connected Documents

Documents on an intranet are connected. Employees can select highlighted text or images, called hyperlinks or links, in one document to display a related document.

Software

The software used to exchange information on an intranet, such as a Web browser or e-mail program, is the same as the software used to exchange information on the Internet.

CHAPTER 10

THE INTERNET AND THE WORLD WIDE WEB

How can I get connected to the Internet and browse the Web? This chapter will help you get started.

INTRODUCTION TO THE INTERNET

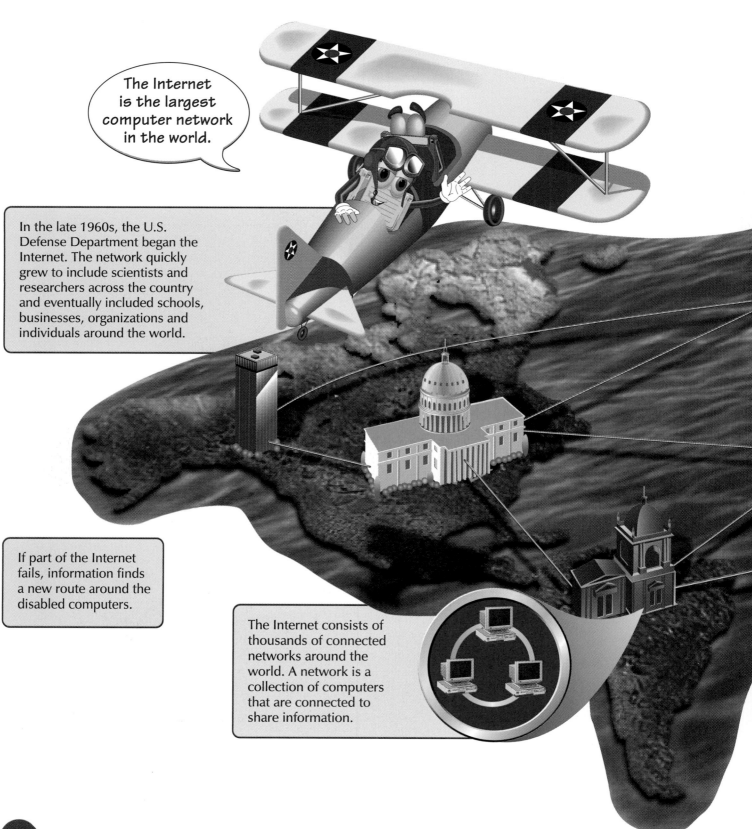

The Internet is the largest computer network in the world.

In the late 1960s, the U.S. Defense Department began the Internet. The network quickly grew to include scientists and researchers across the country and eventually included schools, businesses, organizations and individuals around the world.

If part of the Internet fails, information finds a new route around the disabled computers.

The Internet consists of thousands of connected networks around the world. A network is a collection of computers that are connected to share information.

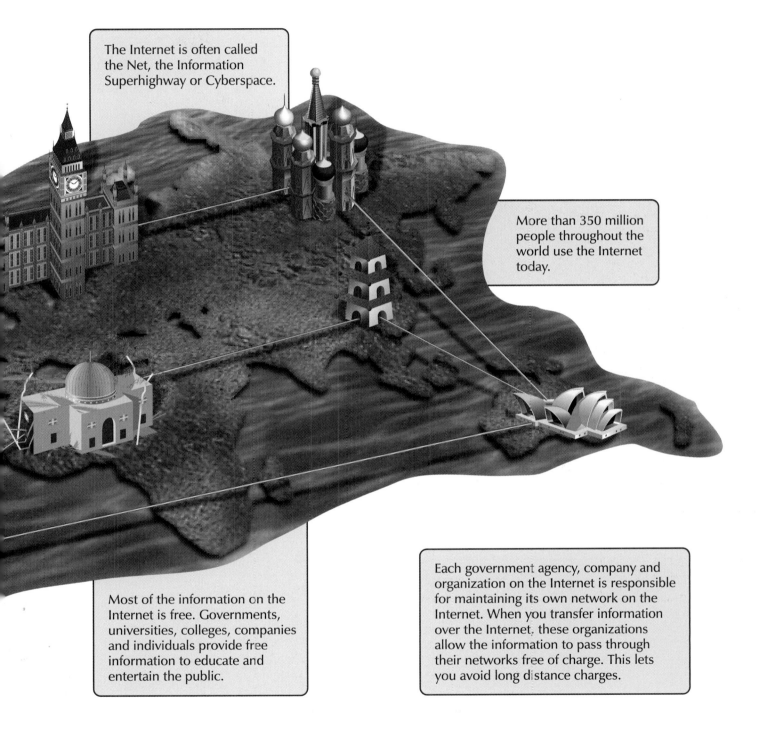

The Internet is often called the Net, the Information Superhighway or Cyberspace.

More than 350 million people throughout the world use the Internet today.

Most of the information on the Internet is free. Governments, universities, colleges, companies and individuals provide free information to educate and entertain the public.

Each government agency, company and organization on the Internet is responsible for maintaining its own network on the Internet. When you transfer information over the Internet, these organizations allow the information to pass through their networks free of charge. This lets you avoid long distance charges.

WHAT THE INTERNET OFFERS

ELECTRONIC MAIL

Electronic mail (e-mail) is the most popular feature on the Internet. You can exchange electronic mail with people around the world, including friends, colleagues, family members, customers and even people you meet on the Internet. Electronic mail is fast, easy, inexpensive and saves paper.

INFORMATION

The Internet gives you access to information on any subject imaginable. This makes the Internet a valuable research tool. You can review newspapers, magazines, academic papers, dictionaries, encyclopedias, travel guides, government documents, television show transcripts, recipes, job listings, airline schedules and much more.

ENTERTAINMENT

The Internet offers many different forms of entertainment, such as radio broadcasts, video clips and music. You can find pictures from the latest films, watch live interviews with your favorite celebrities and listen to music before it is available in stores. You can also play interactive games with other people around the world.

DISCUSSION GROUPS

You can join discussion groups on the Internet to meet people around the world with similar interests. You can ask questions, discuss problems and read interesting stories. There are thousands of discussion groups on topics such as the environment, food, humor, music, politics and sports.

CHAT

The chat feature allows you to exchange typed messages with another person on the Internet. A message you send will instantly appear on the other person's computer. You can chat with one person at a time or with a group of people.

PROGRAMS

You can find programs to use on your computer, including word processors, drawing programs and games. You can also obtain programs, called shareware, that you can try for a limited time. If you like the program and want to continue using it, you must pay the author of the program.

ONLINE SHOPPING

You can order goods and services on the Internet without leaving your desk. You can purchase items such as books, computer programs, flowers, music CDs, pizza, stocks and used cars.

You need equipment, software and an Internet service provider to connect to the Internet.

COMPUTER

You can use any type of computer, such as an IBM-compatible or Macintosh computer, to connect to the Internet.

SOFTWARE

Most computers come with software to help you set up the computer to access the Internet. For example, computers that come with Windows Me include the Internet Connection Wizard.

You also need software, such as a Web browser, to access information on the Internet. Most new computers come with this software installed.

MODEM OR HIGH-SPEED CONNECTION

You need a modem or high-speed Internet connection to connect to the Internet. For more information, see pages 44 to 49.

INTERNET SERVICE PROVIDER

An Internet Service Provider (ISP) is a company that gives you access to the Internet for a fee. Make sure you choose an ISP with a local telephone number to avoid long distance charges.

Many ISPs offer you a certain number of hours per month for a set fee. If you exceed the total number of hours, you are usually charged for every extra hour you use the provider. Some ISPs offer unlimited access to the Internet for a set fee.

Commercial Online Service

A commercial online service is a type of ISP that offers an enormous amount of well-organized information and services such as daily news, weather reports and chat rooms. America Online (AOL) is the most popular commercial online service.

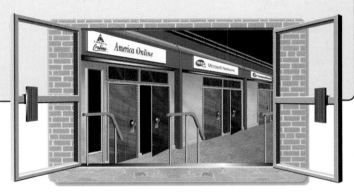

OTHER WAYS TO CONNECT

You can use some wireless devices, such as cellular telephones or handheld computers, to connect to the Internet so you can access information and exchange electronic mail.

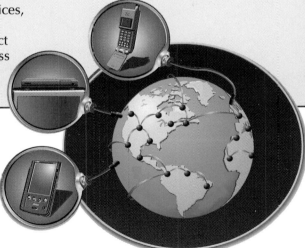

There are also Internet television terminals that allow you to access the Internet using your television. An Internet television terminal is also called a set-top box.

INTRODUCTION TO THE WEB

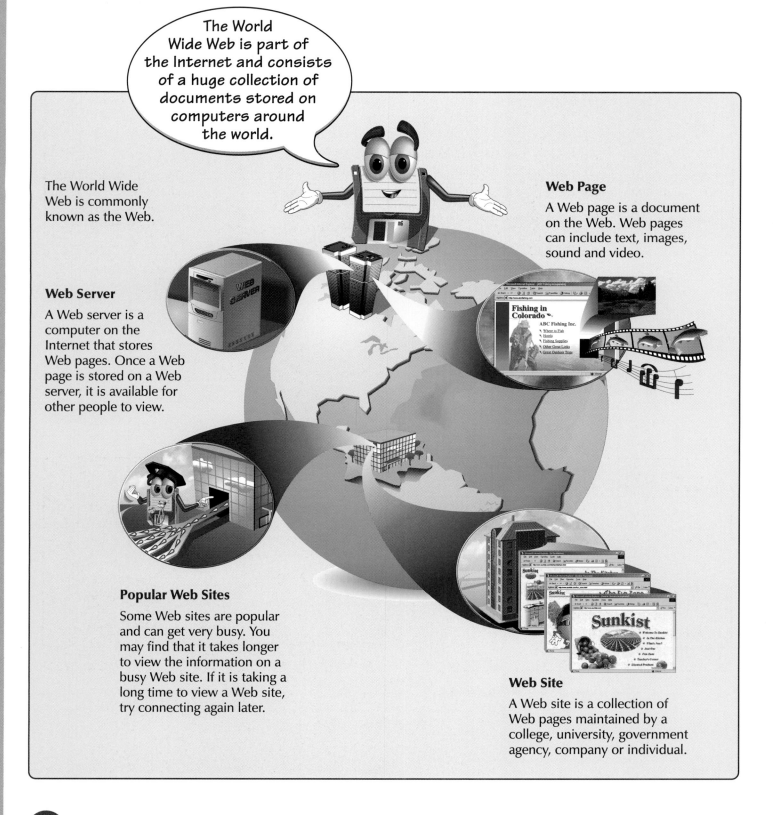

The World Wide Web is part of the Internet and consists of a huge collection of documents stored on computers around the world.

The World Wide Web is commonly known as the Web.

Web Server

A Web server is a computer on the Internet that stores Web pages. Once a Web page is stored on a Web server, it is available for other people to view.

Web Page

A Web page is a document on the Web. Web pages can include text, images, sound and video.

Popular Web Sites

Some Web sites are popular and can get very busy. You may find that it takes longer to view the information on a busy Web site. If it is taking a long time to view a Web site, try connecting again later.

Web Site

A Web site is a collection of Web pages maintained by a college, university, government agency, company or individual.

URL

Each Web page has a unique address, called a Uniform Resource Locator (URL). You can instantly display any Web page if you know its URL.

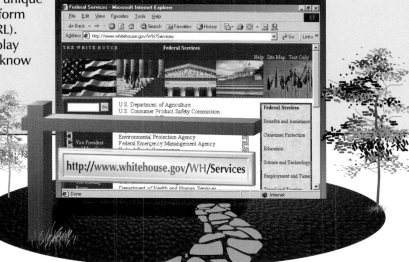

A Web page URL starts with **http** (HyperText Transfer Protocol) and contains the **computer name**, **directory name** and the **name of the Web page**.

HYPERLINKS

Web pages contain highlighted text or images, called hyperlinks or links, that connect to other pages on the Web. Hyperlinks allow you to easily move through a vast amount of information by jumping from one Web page to another. You can select a hyperlink to jump to a Web page located on the same computer or a computer across the city, country or world.

You can easily identify text hyperlinks on a Web page because they appear underlined and in color.

WEB BROWSER

A Web browser is a program that lets you view and explore information on the World Wide Web.

WEB BROWSER SCREEN

Most Web browsers have a similar look and feel.

■ This area displays the address of the page you are currently viewing.

■ This area displays a toolbar to help you quickly perform common tasks.

■ This area displays a Web page.

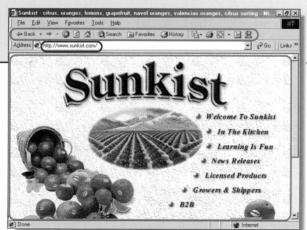

HOME PAGE

The home page is the Web page that appears each time you start your Web browser.

You can choose any page on the Web as your home page. Make sure you choose a home page that provides a good starting point for exploring the Web.

POPULAR WEB BROWSERS

Microsoft Internet Explorer

Microsoft Internet Explorer is currently the most popular Web browser. Internet Explorer comes with the Windows operating systems and the latest version of the Macintosh operating system, Mac OS X.

You can also obtain Internet Explorer free of charge at the following Web site: www.microsoft.com/windows/ie

Netscape Navigator

Netscape Navigator is a Web browser that is available for computers running the Windows, Macintosh, UNIX or Linux operating systems.

You can obtain Netscape Navigator free of charge at the following Web site: www.netscape.com

WEB BROWSER FEATURES

Bookmarks

Most Web browsers have a feature called bookmarks or favorites. This feature lets you store the addresses of Web pages you frequently visit. Bookmarks save you from having to remember and constantly retype your favorite Web page addresses.

History List

When you are browsing through pages on the World Wide Web, it can be difficult to keep track of the locations of pages you have visited. Most Web browsers include a history list that allows you to quickly return to any Web page you have recently visited.

MULTIMEDIA ON THE WEB

Web pages commonly use multimedia—a combination of text, images, sound and video or animation—to entertain visitors and attract attention to information.

There are many specialized types of multimedia used on the Web.

MP3

MP3 is a sound format used to transfer CD-quality music over the Internet.

Some recording artists distribute their music in MP3 format on the Web. There are many Web sites that allow you to download, or copy, MP3 files to your computer. You can find MP3 files at the following Web sites:

www.emusic.com
www.mp3.com
www.mp3place.com

USING MP3

An MP3 player is software you can use to play MP3 files on your computer. Winamp is a popular MP3 player available at the www.winamp.com Web site.

There is also software available that allows you to record MP3 files onto a CD that you can play in a CD player. For example, Nero by Ahead Software is available at the www.nero.com Web site.

STREAMING MULTIMEDIA

Streaming multimedia is a system that lets you hear or view continuous sound or video on the Web, such as a live concert or sporting event.

You must have a streaming multimedia player to play streaming multimedia on the Web. You can find streaming multimedia players at the following Web sites:

RealPlayer
www.real.com

QuickTime
www.apple.com/quicktime

WEB PAGE ENHANCEMENTS

Most new Web browsers can display Java, JavaScript and ActiveX enhancements.

Java

Java is a complex programming language that allows people to create animated and interactive Web pages. Java-enhanced Web pages can display animation and moving text, play music and much more.

JavaScript

JavaScript is a simple programming language that is used mainly for Web page enhancements, such as displaying scrolling messages and fading-in Web pages.

ActiveX

ActiveX is a technology used to improve Web pages. For example, people can use ActiveX to add pop-up menus that instantly display a list of options on a Web page.

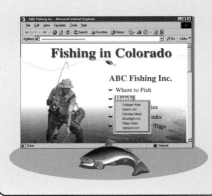

A Web portal is a Web site that provides an excellent starting point for exploring the Internet.

Yahoo! is the most popular Web portal. You can visit Yahoo! at www.yahoo.com.

Other popular Web portals include:
www.excite.com
www.go.com
www.lycos.com

FIND INFORMATION

All Web portals let you type a word or phrase to quickly search for information of interest on the Web. You can also browse through categories, such as business or sports, to find information that interests you.

FREE SERVICES

Most Web portals offer free e-mail services, which allow you to send and receive e-mail from any computer that has access to the Web.

Web portals also offer free services such as up-to-date news headlines, telephone and e-mail directories, shopping services, maps, chat rooms, games, stock quotes and sports scores.

SHOPPING ON THE WEB

You can buy products and services on the Web without ever leaving your desk.

There are thousands of products you can buy on the Web, such as clothing, office supplies, computer programs and food. The Web is also a great source for purchasing rare items, such as out-of-print books.

SHOPPING WEB SITES

Many companies have Web sites where you can view and buy their products. There are also Web sites that offer a variety of products from many different companies. For example, you can find products such as lawn furniture, kitchen accessories, books and video games at:

www.walmart.com

AUCTIONS

You can find auctions on the Web that allow you to bid on products such as computers, jewelry, gifts and much more. eBay is a popular auction Web site located at:

www.ebay.com

SECURE WEB SITES

You can safely transfer confidential information, such as credit card numbers and bank records, to a secure site on the Web. The address of a secure site usually starts with https rather than http.

CHILDREN AND THE WEB

Children should be carefully monitored when browsing the World Wide Web.

Most of the information on the Web is meant to educate or entertain people, but some sites may contain material that is inappropriate for children.

TYPES OF INAPPROPRIATE INFORMATION

Pictures

There are many sites on the Web that display pictures meant for adult users. Most adult-oriented sites require verification that users are adults, but the sites often display sample pictures on the first page of the Web site.

Documents

There are many documents on the Web describing everything from causing mischief at school to making explosives. These types of documents may appeal to teenagers and may be found at Web sites distributing banned or censored books. These Web sites generally do not have any restrictions on who can access the documents.

HOW TO RESTRICT ACCESS

Adult Supervision

Constant adult supervision is the best way to ensure that children do not access inappropriate information on the Web.

Before each Web browsing session, the adult and child should decide on the purpose of the session, such as researching a school project. This will help set ground rules for browsing and make the time spent on the Web more productive.

Browser Restrictions

Some Web browsers allow you to restrict the information children can access on the Web. Many Web sites are rated using a system similar to the one used to rate television shows and films.

You can set your Web browser to allow access only to Web sites that comply with specific ratings.

Restriction Programs

You can buy programs that let you restrict access to certain Web sites. Most of these programs provide a frequently updated list of Web sites considered inappropriate for children.

You can purchase restriction programs at the following Web sites:

Cyber Patrol
www.cyberpatrol.com

Net Nanny
www.netnanny.com

CREATE AND PUBLISH WEB PAGES

You can create and publish Web pages to share information with people around the world.

Individuals publish Web pages to share their favorite pictures, hobbies and interests. Companies publish Web pages to promote their businesses, advertise products and publicize job openings.

ORGANIZE IDEAS

Before you start creating Web pages, decide what ideas you will discuss and how the ideas relate to one another. Break up your information so you discuss one major idea on each Web page. You may find it helpful to first sketch the design of your Web pages on paper.

HTML

HyperText Markup Language (HTML) is a computer code used to create Web pages. There are many programs available, called visual editors, which can help you create Web pages without having to learn HTML. You can obtain visual editors at the following Web sites:

Microsoft FrontPage
www.microsoft.com/frontpage

HoTMetaL PRO
www.softquad.com

HYPERLINKS

You can add hyperlinks, or links, to your Web pages. Hyperlinks are highlighted text or images that connect to other pages on the Web. Hyperlinks are one of the most important features of Web pages since they let people move easily through information of interest.

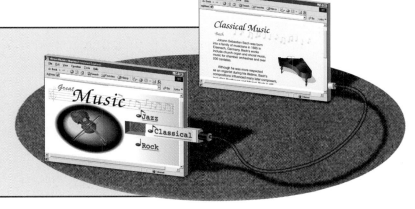

IMAGES

You can add images to your Web pages to enhance the appearance of the pages. You can create your own images, use a scanner to scan images into your computer, buy images at computer stores or find images on the Internet. Make sure you have permission to use any images you did not create yourself.

PUBLISH YOUR WEB PAGES

When you finish creating your Web pages, you can publish the pages by transferring them to a Web server. The company that gives you access to the Internet usually offers space on its Web server where you can publish your Web pages.

CHAPTER 11

ELECTRONIC MAIL AND MAILING LISTS

How can I communicate with other people on the Internet? This chapter introduces you to electronic mail and mailing lists.

INTRODUCTION TO E-MAIL

You can exchange electronic mail (e-mail) with people around the world.

E-mail is a fast, economical and convenient way to send messages to family, friends and colleagues.

E-MAIL PROGRAMS

An e-mail program lets you send, receive and manage your e-mail messages.

Popular e-mail programs include Microsoft Outlook Express, Netscape Messenger and Qualcomm's Eudora.

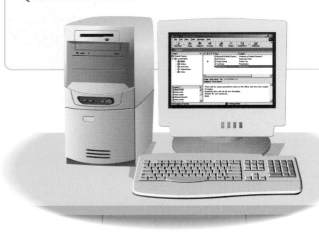

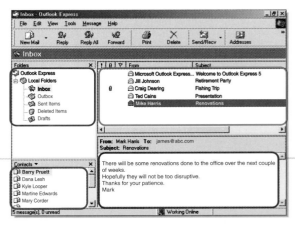

Outlook Express

■ This area displays the folders that contain your e-mail messages.

■ This area displays a list of all your e-mail messages.

■ This area displays the contents of a single e-mail message.

■ This area displays a list of your contacts.

E-MAIL ADDRESSES

You can send a message to anyone around the world if you know the person's e-mail address.

mvickers@sales.abc.com

An e-mail address defines the location of an individual's mailbox on the Internet.

PARTS OF AN E-MAIL ADDRESS

An e-mail address consists of two parts separated by the @ ("at") symbol. An e-mail address cannot contain spaces.

mvickers@sales.abc.com

■ The **user name** is the name of the person's account. This can be a real name or a nickname.

■ The **domain name** is the location of the person's account on the Internet. Periods (.) separate the various parts of the domain name.

ORGANIZATION OR COUNTRY

The last few characters in an e-mail address usually indicate the type of organization the person belongs to or the country the person lives in.

ORGANIZATION		COUNTRY	
com	commercial	au	Australia
edu	education	ca	Canada
gov	government	ie	Ireland
mil	military	it	Italy
net	network	jp	Japan
org	organization (often non-profit)	uk	United Kingdom

CREATE A MESSAGE

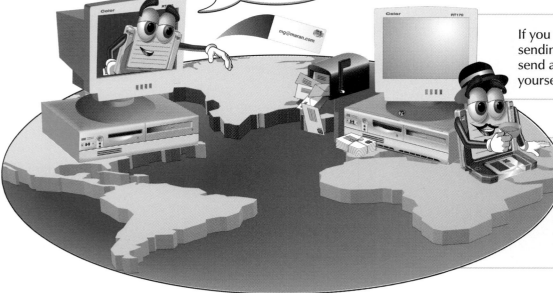

> You can send a message to exchange ideas or request information.

If you want to practice sending a message, send a message to yourself.

When you send a message, do not assume the person will read the message right away. Some people may not regularly check their messages.

COST

Once you pay a service provider for a connection to the Internet, there is no charge for sending and receiving e-mail. You do not have to pay extra even if you send a long message or the message travels around the world.

Exchanging e-mail can save you money on long distance calls. The next time you are about to pick up the telephone, consider sending an e-mail message instead.

WRITING STYLE

Make sure every message you send is clear, concise and contains no spelling or grammar errors. Also make sure the message will not be misinterpreted. For example, the reader may not realize a statement is meant to be sarcastic.

MESSAGE TIPS

Smileys

You can use special characters, called smileys or emoticons, to express emotions in messages. These characters resemble human faces if you turn them sideways.

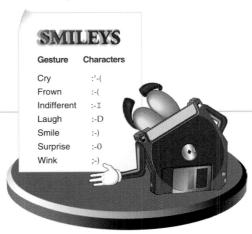

SMILEYS

Gesture	Characters
Cry	:'-(
Frown	:-(
Indifferent	:-I
Laugh	:-D
Smile	:-)
Surprise	:-0
Wink	;-)

Abbreviations

Abbreviations are commonly used in messages to save time typing.

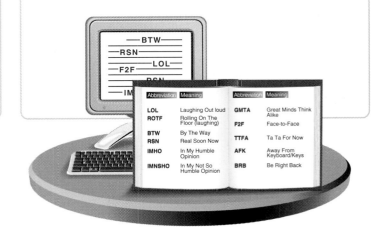

Abbreviation	Meaning	Abbreviation	Meaning
LOL	Laughing Out loud	GMTA	Great Minds Think Alike
ROTF	Rolling On The Floor (laughing)	F2F	Face-to-Face
BTW	By The Way	TTFA	Ta Ta For Now
RSN	Real Soon Now	AFK	Away From Keyboard/Keys
IMHO	In My Humble Opinion	BRB	Be Right Back
IMNSHO	In My Not So Humble Opinion		

Shouting

A MESSAGE WRITTEN IN CAPITAL LETTERS IS ANNOYING AND HARD TO READ. THIS IS CALLED SHOUTING.

Always use uppercase and lowercase letters when typing messages.

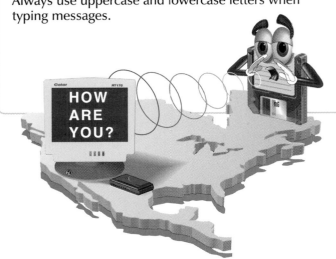

Flame

A flame is an angry or insulting message directed at one person. A flame war is an argument that continues for a while. Avoid starting or participating in flame wars.

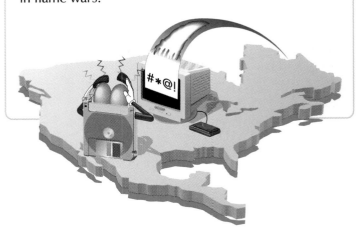

RECEIVE A MESSAGE

You do not have to be at your computer to receive an e-mail message. Your Internet service provider stores the messages you receive in a mailbox. When you check for new messages, you are checking your mailbox on the service provider's computer. Make sure you regularly check for messages.

You can use most computers on the Internet to connect to your service provider and retrieve messages. This allows you to check your messages while traveling.

REPLY TO A MESSAGE

You can reply to a message you receive to answer a question, express an opinion or supply additional information.

MESSAGES

REPLIES

When you reply to a message, make sure you include part of the original message. This is called quoting. Quoting helps the reader identify which message you are replying to.

FORWARD A MESSAGE

After reading a message you receive, you can add comments and then send the message to a friend or colleague.

FORWARD TO:
Rick Mason

ADDRESS BOOK

Most e-mail programs provide an address book where you can store the addresses of people you frequently send messages to. An address book saves you from having to type the same addresses over and over again.

SIGNATURE

You can have an e-mail program add information about yourself to the end of every message you send. This prevents you from having to repeatedly type the same information.

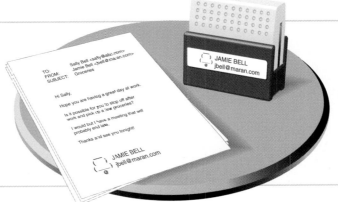

A signature can include your name, e-mail address, occupation or favorite quotation. You can also use plain characters to display simple pictures.

ATTACH A FILE TO A MESSAGE

You can attach a document, image, sound, video or program to a message you are sending. The computer receiving the message must have a program that can display or play the file.

You should try to keep the size of an attached file under 500 KB, since many computers on the Internet take a long time to transfer messages with large attached files.

WEB-BASED E-MAIL

There are several Web sites that allow you to send and receive e-mail on the Web free of charge.

You use your Web browser to send and receive Web-based e-mail. You do not need an e-mail program installed on your computer.

POPULAR WEB-BASED E-MAIL SERVICES

There are several Web-based e-mail services available. You can find popular Web-based e-mail services at the following Web sites:
www.hotmail.com
www.email.com
mail.yahoo.com

WORLDWIDE ACCESS

When you use a Web-based e-mail service, you can access your e-mail from any computer in the world that has access to the Web. Web-based e-mail is useful for people who need to access their e-mail while traveling.

PERMANENT E-MAIL ADDRESS

Using a Web-based e-mail service allows you to obtain an e-mail address that will not change. This lets you keep the same e-mail address even if you switch to a new Internet service provider.

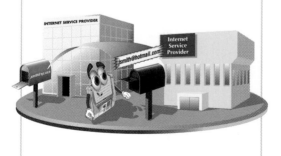

E-MAIL VIRUSES

An e-mail virus is a program that can disrupt the normal operation of a computer.

A virus can cause problems such as displaying unusual messages on the screen or destroying information on the hard drive.

HOW E-MAIL VIRUSES SPREAD

Most e-mail viruses spread to your computer when you open an e-mail attachment containing the virus. You can spread some e-mail viruses to your computer just by opening an infected e-mail message. A virus can spread to other computers if you forward a message containing the virus to other people. Some e-mail viruses can also access your address book and send themselves to the e-mail addresses stored there.

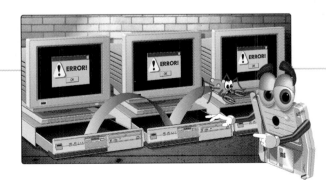

VIRUS PREVENTION

Only open e-mail attachments and e-mail messages sent by people you trust. You should also use a virus scanner to check e-mail messages for viruses. Virus scanner manufacturers regularly release updates that allow their programs to detect the latest known viruses. Make sure your virus scanner is up-to-date.

You can find popular virus scanners at the following Web sites:
www.mcafee.com
www.symantec.com/nav

INTRODUCTION TO MAILING LISTS

A mailing list is a discussion group that uses e-mail to communicate. When a mailing list receives a message, a copy of the message goes to everyone on the mailing list.

There are thousands of mailing lists that cover a wide variety of topics, from aromatherapy to zoology.

You can find mailing lists that discuss a specific topic at the following Web sites: paml.net www.liszt.com

MANUALLY MAINTAINED LISTS

A manually maintained list is managed by a person, who is often referred to as an administrator.

Before you subscribe to a manually maintained list, make sure you find out what information the administrator needs and include the information in your message.

AUTOMATED LISTS

An automated mailing list is managed by a computer program. The three most popular programs for managing automated mailing lists are listproc, listserv and majordomo.

The name of the program that manages the mailing list usually appears in the e-mail address you use to subscribe to the list (example: listserv@LSV.UKY.EDU).

SUBSCRIBE TO A MAILING LIST

Just as you would subscribe to a newspaper or magazine, you can subscribe to a mailing list that interests you. Subscribing adds your e-mail address to the mailing list.

Unsubscribe

If you no longer want to receive messages from a mailing list, you can unsubscribe from the mailing list at any time. Unsubscribing removes your e-mail address from the mailing list.

MAILING LIST ADDRESSES

Each mailing list has two addresses. Make sure you send your messages to the appropriate address.

Mailing List Address

The mailing list address receives messages intended for the entire mailing list. This is the address you use to send messages you want all the people on the list to receive. Do not send subscription or unsubscription requests to the mailing list address.

Administrative Address

The administrative address receives messages dealing with administrative issues. This is the address you use to subscribe to or unsubscribe from a mailing list.

CHAPTER 12

NEWSGROUPS AND CHAT

What is a newsgroup? How can I chat with other people on the Internet? Find the answers to these questions and more in this chapter.

rec.autos

INTRODUCTION TO NEWSGROUPS

> A newsgroup is a discussion group that allows people with common interests to communicate with each other.

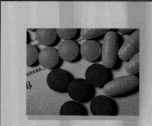

There are thousands of newsgroups on every subject imaginable. Each newsgroup discusses a particular topic such as jobs offered, puzzles or medicine.

Usenet, short for Users' Network, refers to all the computers that distribute newsgroup information.

MESSAGES

A newsgroup can contain hundreds or thousands of messages.

Message

A message is information that an individual posts, or sends, to a newsgroup. A message can be a few lines of text or the length of a book. Messages are also called articles.

I have two weeks vacation coming up. Any suggestions for a fun place to spend it?

I had a great time in Hawaii.

I really enjoyed Mexico.

Get on a ship! A cruise is very relaxing!

Thread

A thread is a message and all replies to the message. A thread may include an initial question and the responses from other readers.

NEWSGROUP NAMES

The name of a newsgroup describes the type of information discussed in the newsgroup. A newsgroup name consists of two or more words, separatedby periods (.).

The first word describes the main topic (example: rec for recreation). Each of the following words narrows the topic.

NEWSREADER

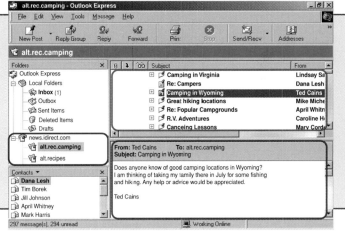

A newsreader is a program that lets you read and post messages to newsgroups. Microsoft Outlook Express comes with a built-in newsreader. Other popular newsreaders include MicroPlanet Gravity and Forté Free Agent.

■ This area displays a list of newsgroups.

■ This area displays a list of all the messages in the selected newsgroup.

■ This area displays the contents of a single message.

NEWS SERVER

A news server is a computer that stores newsgroup messages. News servers are maintained by Internet service providers. The newsgroups available to you depend on your service provider. Your service provider may limit the available newsgroups to save valuable storage space.

SUBSCRIBE TO A NEWSGROUP

You can subscribe to a newsgroup you want to read on a regular basis.

If you no longer want to read the messages in a newsgroup, you can unsubscribe from the newsgroup at any time.

NEWSGROUP CATEGORIES

Newsgroups are divided into sections, or categories. The newsgroups in each category discuss the same general topic.

Main Newsgroup Categories

Category	Topic	Example
alt	General interest	alt.fans.actors
biz	Business	biz.entrepreneurs
comp	Computers	comp.security.misc
misc	Miscellaneous	misc.books.technical
rec	Recreation and hobbies	rec.food.recipes
sci	Science	sci.physics
soc	Social (culture and politics)	soc.history
talk	Debate	talk.politics.misc

There is often more than one newsgroup for a topic. For example, the topics discussed in the alt.books.reviews newsgroup are similar to the topics discussed in rec.arts.books. If you are interested in a specific topic, you may want to subscribe to all the newsgroups that discuss the topic.

POST A MESSAGE

You can post, or send, a new message to a newsgroup to ask a question or express an opinion. Thousands of people around the world may read a message you post.

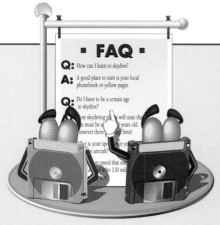

Read the FAQ

Before posting a message to a newsgroup, make sure you read the newsgroup's FAQ. A FAQ (Frequently Asked Questions) is a document that contains a list of questions and answers that often appear in a newsgroup. The FAQ is designed to prevent new readers from asking questions that have already been answered.

REPLY TO A MESSAGE

You can reply to a message to answer a question, express an opinion or supply additional information. When you reply to a message, make sure you include part of the original message. This is called quoting. Quoting helps readers identify which message you are replying to.

Send a Private Reply

You can send a reply to the author of a message, the entire newsgroup or both. If your reply would not be of interest to others in a newsgroup or if you want to send a private reply, send a message only to the author of the message.

INTRODUCTION TO CHAT

You can instantly communicate with people around the world by typing back and forth. This is called chatting.

Chatting is one of the most popular features of the Internet.

You can chat with family, friends and colleagues in other cities, states or countries without paying long distance telephone charges.

TEXT-BASED CHAT

Text-based chat is the oldest and most popular type of chat on the Internet. You can have conversations with one or more people. When chatting, the text you send immediately appears on the screen of each person participating in the conversation.

MULTIMEDIA CHAT

Multimedia chat lets you have voice conversations and communicate through live video over the Internet. You need equipment such as a microphone, speakers and a video camera to participate in multimedia chat. Since sound and video transfer over the Internet more slowly than text, you should also have a high-speed connection to the Internet to use multimedia chat.

You can obtain Microsoft NetMeeting, a popular multimedia chat program, at the www.microsoft.com/netmeeting Web site.

INTERNET RELAY CHAT

Internet Relay Chat (IRC) is a popular chatting system on the Internet. You can join a chat group, or channel, on IRC. Each channel focuses on a specific topic, such as music or politics.

You need an IRC program to participate in IRC chats. You can obtain an IRC program at the www.mirc.com Web site.

WEB-BASED CHAT

There are sites on the Web that let you chat with other people. For example, the www.talkcity.com Web site offers Web-based chat. Usually, all you need to participate in Web-based chat is a Web browser.

INSTANT MESSAGING

Instant messaging lets you chat privately with another person on the Internet. You need a special program to participate in instant messaging. You must use the same instant messaging program as the people you want to exchange messages with.

You can find popular instant messaging programs at the following Web sites:

MSN Messenger Service
messenger.msn.com

AOL Instant Messenger
aim.aol.com

INDEX

U

UDMA (Ultra Direct Memory Access), 85
UNIX, 125, 136-137
unsubscribe, from mailing list, 209
update Windows, in Windows Me, 133
upgrade computer, 19
UPS (Uninterruptible Power Supply), 13
URL (Uniform Resource Locator), 187
USB (Universal Serial Bus) port, 15, 66-67
    in Macintosh computer, 161
Usenet (Users' Network). *See* newsgroup
user
    account, in Linux, 139
    name
        in e-mail address, 201
        in network, 176
utility
    program, in MS-DOS, 127
    software, 118-119
UTP (Unshielded Twisted Pair) cable, 171

V

V.90, modem standard, 46
version
    software, 109
    UNIX, 136
ViaVoice, 119
video
    capabilities, in Macintosh computer, 162
    capture, using TV tuner card, 55
    card, 17, 36-43
        memory, 41
        TV tuner, 54
    editing, software, 62
    on Web, 190
videoconferencing
    in network, 170
    using Web camera, 63
virtual memory, 71
virus, 87
    in e-mail message, 207
    scanner
        in e-mail, 207
        program, 87
VirusScan, 118
voice capabilities, in modem, 45

W

WAN (Wide Area Network), 168
watts, 13
Wavetable synthesis, 53
Web
    and children, 194-195
    browser, 188-189
        restrictions, 195

    camera, 63
    introduction. 186-187
    multimedia, 190-191
    page, 186
        add image, 197
        create, 196-197
        enhancement, 191
        publish, 196-197
    portal, 192
    server, 186
    shopping online, 193
    site, 186
        secure, 193
Web-based
    chat, 217
    e-mail, 206
window, 128
Windows, 125
    2000, 135
    3.1, 128
    95, 129
    98, 130-131
    CE, 155
    Explorer, 129
    key, 26
    Me (Millennium Edition), 132-133
    Media Player, 132
    Movie Maker, 132
    NT, 134
    Update, 133
WinFax Pro, 119
WinZip, 119
wireless modem, in handheld computer, 154
word processor, 110-111
    in application suite, 117
World Wide Web. *See* Web
write-protect floppy disk, 91
WYSIWYG (What You See Is What You Get) display, 158

Z

Zip drive, 104

Read Less, Learn More™

Visual

Simplified®

Simply the Easiest Way to Learn

For visual learners who are brand-new to a topic and want to be shown, not told, how to solve a problem in a friendly, approachable way.

All *Simplified*® books feature friendly Disk characters who demonstrate and explain the purpose of each task.

Title	ISBN	Price
America Online® Simplified®, 2nd Ed.	0-7645-3433-5	$24.99
Computers Simplified®, 4th Ed.	0-7645-6042-5	$24.99
Creating Web Pages with HTML Simplified®, 2nd Ed.	0-7645-6067-0	$24.99
Excel 97 Simplified®	0-7645-6022-0	$24.99
Excel for Windows® 95 Simplified®	1-56884-682-7	$19.99
FrontPage® 2000® Simplified®	0-7645-3450-5	$24.99
Internet and World Wide Web Simplified®, 3rd Ed.	0-7645-3409-2	$24.99
Lotus® 1-2-3® Release 5 for Windows® Simplified®	1-56884-670-3	$19.99
Microsoft® Access 2000 Simplified®	0-7645-6058-1	$24.99
Microsoft® Excel 2000 Simplified®	0-7645-6053-0	$24.99
Microsoft® Office 2000 Simplified®	0-7645-6052-2	$29.99
Microsoft® Word 2000 Simplified®	0-7645-6054-9	$24.99
More Windows® 95 Simplified®	1-56884-689-4	$19.99
More Windows® 98 Simplified®	0-7645-6037-9	$24.99
Office 97 Simplified®	0-7645-6009-3	$29.99
PC Upgrade and Repair Simplified®	0-7645-6049-2	$24.99
Windows® 95 Simplified®	1-56884-662-2	$19.99
Windows® 98 Simplified®	0-7645-6030-1	$24.99
Windows® 2000 Professional Simplified®	0-7645-3422-X	$24.99
Windows® Me Millennium Edition Simplified®	0-7645-3494-7	$24.99
Word 97 Simplified®	0-7645-6011-5	$24.99

Over 10 million *Visual* books in print!

with these full-color Visual™ guides

The Fast and Easy Way to Learn

Discover how to use what you learn with "Teach Yourself" tips

For visual learners who want to guide themselves through the basics of any technology topic. *Teach Yourself VISUALLY offers more expanded coverage than our bestselling Simplified series.*

Title	ISBN	Price
Teach Yourself Access 97 VISUALLY™	0-7645-6026-3	$29.99
Teach Yourself Computers and the Internet VISUALLY™, 2nd Ed.	0-7645-6041-7	$29.99
Teach Yourself FrontPage® 2000 VISUALLY™	0-7645-3451-3	$29.99
Teach Yourself HTML VISUALLY™	0-7645-3423-8	$29.99
Teach Yourself the Internet and World Wide Web VISUALLY™, 2nd Ed.	0-7645-3410-6	$29.99
Teach Yourself Microsoft® Access 2000 VISUALLY™	0-7645-6059-X	$29.99
Teach Yourself Microsoft® Excel 97 VISUALLY™	0-7645-6063-8	$29.99
Teach Yourself Microsoft® Excel 2000 VISUALLY™	0-7645-6056-5	$29.99
Teach Yourself Microsoft® Office 2000 VISUALLY™	0-7645-6051-4	$29.99
Teach Yourself Microsoft® PowerPoint® 97 VISUALLY™	0-7645-6062-X	$29.99
Teach Yourself Microsoft® PowerPoint® 2000 VISUALLY™	0-7645-6060-3	$29.99
Teach Yourself More Windows® 98 VISUALLY™	0-7645-6044-1	$29.99
Teach Yourself Netscape Navigator® 4 VISUALLY™	0-7645-6028-X	$29.99
Teach Yourself Networking VISUALLY™	0-7645-6023-9	$29.99
Teach Yourself Office 97 VISUALLY™	0-7645-6018-2	$29.99
Teach Yourself Red Hat® Linux® VISUALLY™	0-7645-3430-0	$29.99
Teach Yourself VISUALLY™ Dreamweaver® 3	0-7645-3470-X	$29.99
Teach Yourself VISUALLY™ Flash™ 5	0-7645-3540-4	$29.99
Teach Yourself VISUALLY™ iMac™	0-7645-3453-X	$29.99
Teach Yourself VISUALLY™ Investing Online	0-7645-3459-9	$29.99
Teach Yourself VISUALLY™ Windows® Me Millennium Edition	0-7645-3495-5	$29.99
Teach Yourself VISUALLY™ Windows® 2000 Server	0-7645-3428-9	$29.99
Teach Yourself Windows® 95 VISUALLY™	0-7645-6001-8	$29.99
Teach Yourself Windows® 98 VISUALLY™	0-7645-6025-5	$29.99
Teach Yourself Windows® 2000 Professional VISUALLY	0-7645-6040-9	$29.99
Teach Yourself Word® 97 VISUALLY™	0-7645-6032-8	$29.99

The Visual™ series is available wherever books are sold, or call **1-800-762-2974.** *Outside the US, call* **317-572-3993**

ORDER FORM

IDG BOOKS ®

TRADE & INDIVIDUAL ORDERS

Phone: **(800) 762-2974**
or **(317) 572-3993**
(8 a.m.–6 p.m., CST, weekdays)
FAX : **(800) 550-2747**
or **(317) 572-4002**

EDUCATIONAL ORDERS & DISCOUNTS

Phone: **(800) 434-2086**
(8:30 a.m.–5:00 p.m., CST, weekdays)
FAX : **(317) 572-4005**

CORPORATE ORDERS FOR 3-D VISUAL™ SERIES

Phone: **(800) 469-6616**
(8 a.m.–5 p.m., EST, weekdays)
FAX : **(905) 890-9434**

Qty	ISBN	Title	Price	Total

Shipping & Handling Charges

	Description	First book	Each add'l. book	Total
Domestic	Normal	$4.50	$1.50	$
	Two Day Air	$8.50	$2.50	$
	Overnight	$18.00	$3.00	$
International	Surface	$8.00	$8.00	$
	Airmail	$16.00	$16.00	$
	DHL Air	$17.00	$17.00	$

Subtotal _____

*CA residents add
applicable sales tax* _____

*IN, MA and MD
residents add
5% sales tax* _____

*IL residents add
6.25% sales tax* _____

*RI residents add
7% sales tax* _____

*TX residents add
8.25% sales tax* _____

Shipping _____

Total _____

Ship to:

Name _____

Address _____

Company _____

City/State/Zip _____

Daytime Phone _____

Payment: ☐ Check to IDG Books (US Funds Only)
☐ Visa ☐ Mastercard ☐ American Express

Card # _____ Exp. _____ Signature _____

maranGraphics™